STRUM *Together*

Gospel Songs & Hymns

T0086834

PREFACE

Learning to play a musical instrument is one of the most satisfying experiences a person can have. Being able to play along with other musicians makes that even more rewarding. This collection of gospel songs and hymns is designed to make it easy to enjoy the fun of gathering with friends and family to make music together.

The selections in this book include a variety of songs drawn from traditional gospel songs and hymns. These songs will provide fun opportunities to make music with other players. The music for each song displays the chord diagrams for five instruments: ukulele, baritone ukulele, guitar, mandolin and banjo. The chord diagrams indicate basic, commonly used finger positions. More advanced players can substitute alternate chord formations.

It is easy to find recordings of all these tunes performed by outstanding musicians. Listening can help you understand more about the style as you and your friends play these songs.

Arranged by Mark Phillips

ISBN 978-1-70513-525-9

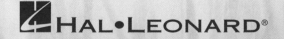

Hal•LEONARD®

Visit Hal Leonard Online at
www.halleonard.com

Contact us:
Hal Leonard
7777 West Bluemound Road
Milwaukee, WI 53213
Email: info@halleonard.com

In Europe, contact:
Hal Leonard Europe Limited
42 Wigmore Street
Marylebone, London, W1U 2RN
Email: info@halleonardeurope.com

In Australia, contact:
Hal Leonard Australia Pty. Ltd.
4 Lentara Court
Cheltenham, Victoria, 3192 Australia
Email: info@halleonard.com.au

Standard Ukulele

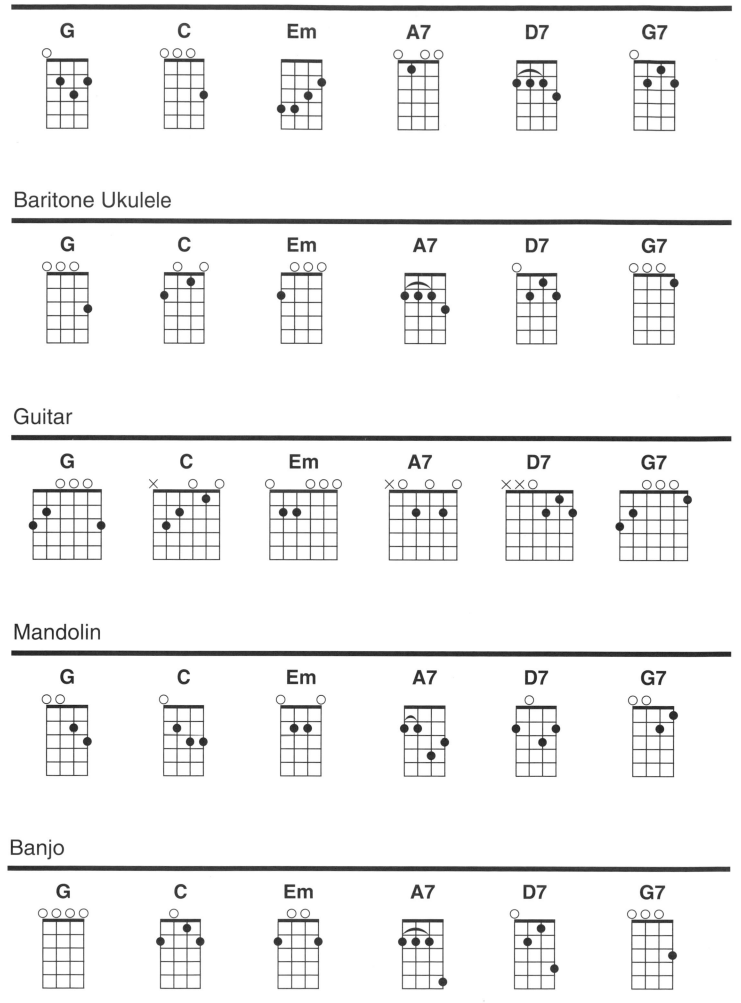

Baritone Ukulele

Guitar

Mandolin

Banjo

Amazing Grace

Words by John Newton
Traditional American Melody

Standard Ukulele

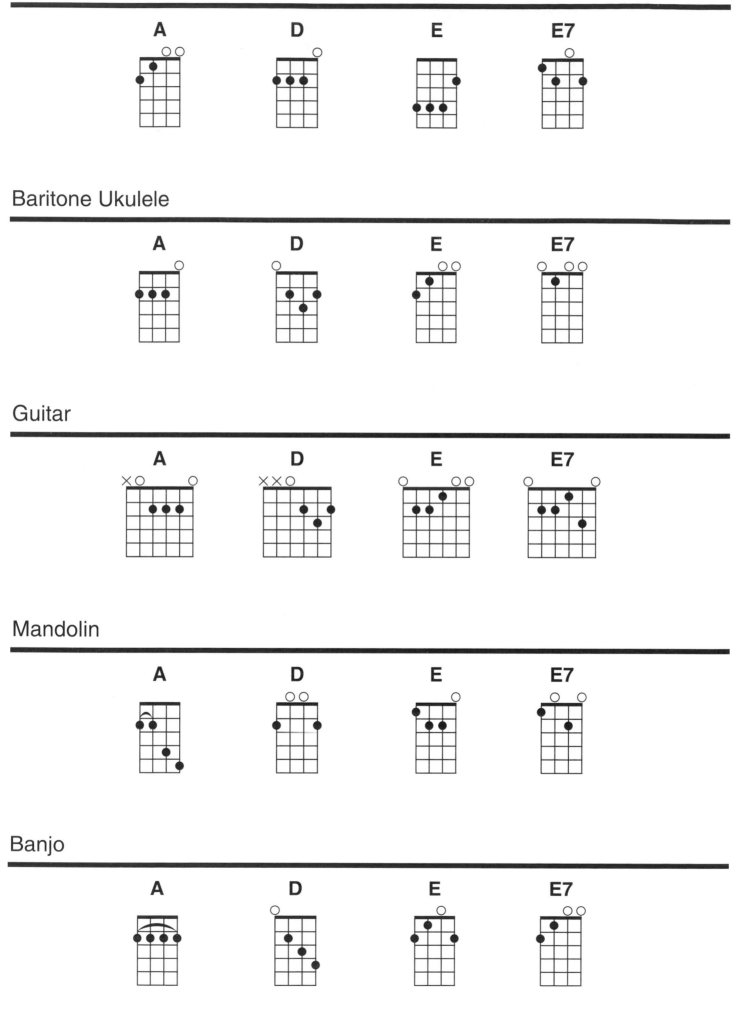

Baritone Ukulele

Guitar

Mandolin

Banjo

Are You Washed in the Blood?

Words and Music by Elisha A. Hoffman

Standard Ukulele

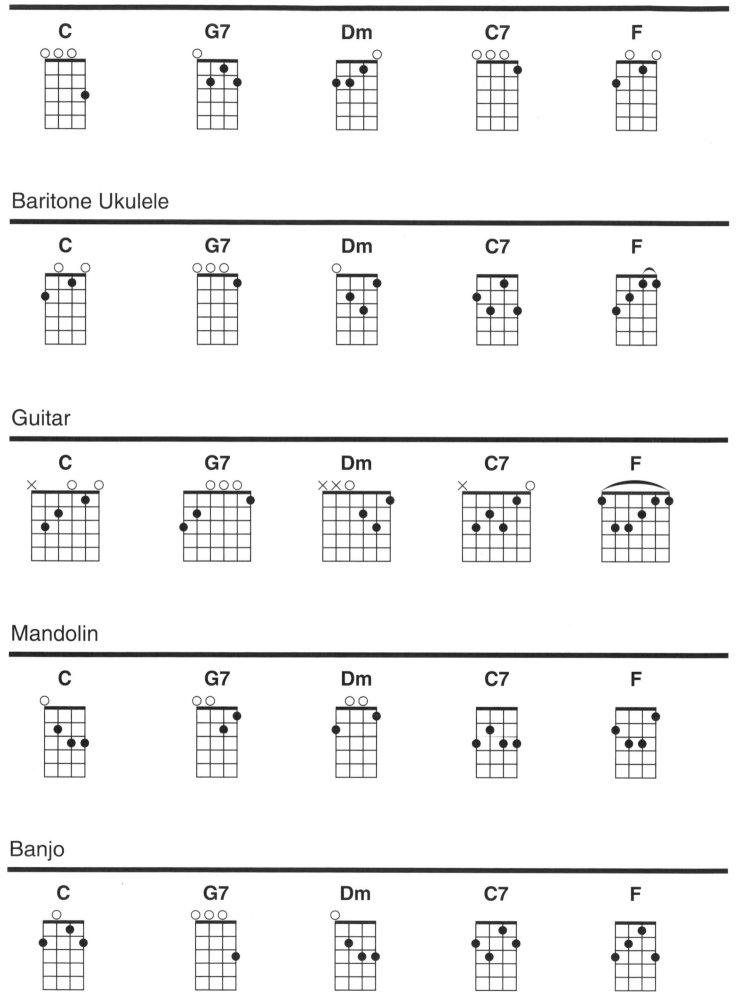

Baritone Ukulele

Guitar

Mandolin

Banjo

At Calvary

Words by William R. Newell
Music by Daniel B. Towner

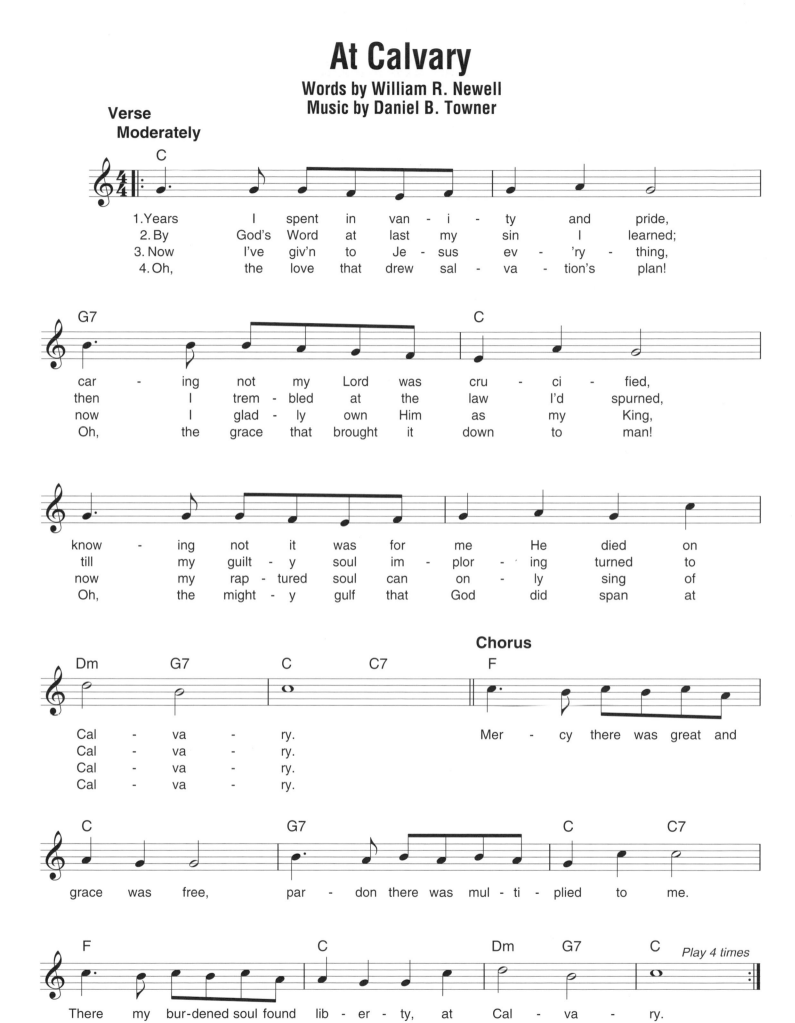

Standard Ukulele

G

C

D

Baritone Ukulele

G

C

D

Guitar

G

C

D

Mandolin

G

C

D

Banjo

G

C

D

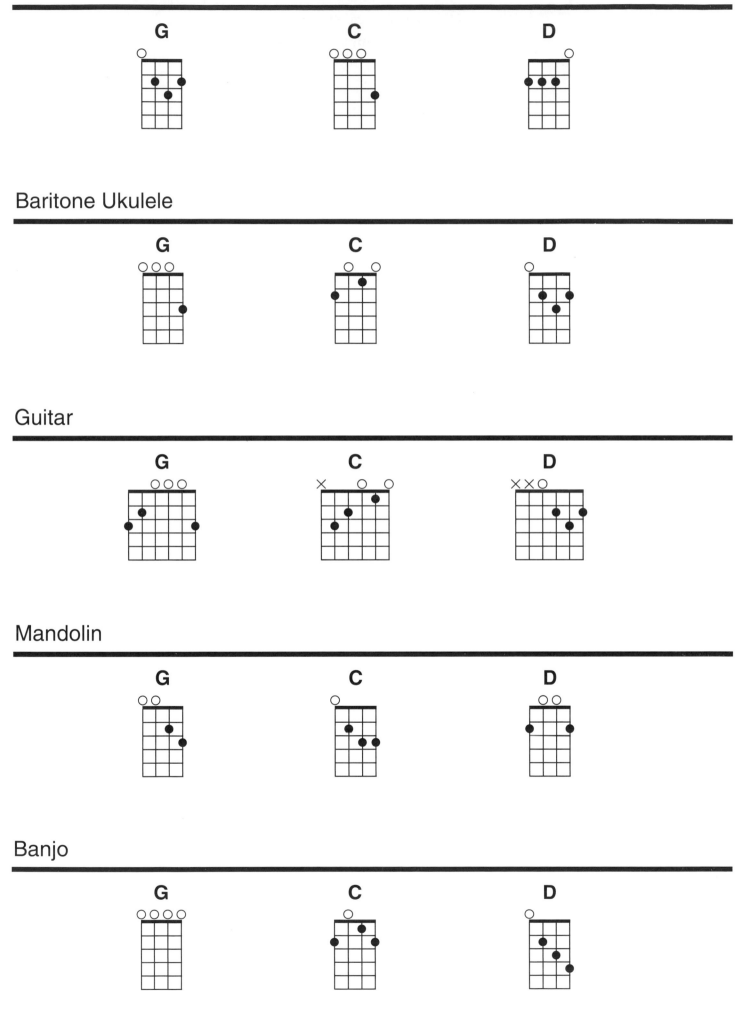

At the Cross

Words by Isaac Watts and Ralph E. Hudson
Music by Ralph E. Hudson

Verse
Moderately

1. A - las! And did my Sav - ior bleed, and did my Sov - 'reign
it for crimes that I have done He groaned up - on the
might the sun in dark - ness hide and shut his glo - ries
might I hide my blush - ing face while Calv - 'ry's cross ap -
drops of grief can ne'er re - pay the debt of love I

die? Would He de - vote that sa - cred head for sin - ners such as
tree? A - maz - ing pit - y! Grace un - known! And love be - yond de -
in, when Christ, the might - y Mak - er, died for man, the crea - ture's
pears, dis - solve my heart in thank - ful - ness and melt mine eyes to
owe. Here, Lord, I give my - self a - way; 'tis all that I can

Chorus

I? }
gree! }
sin. } At the cross, at the cross, where I first __ saw the light and the
tears. }
do! }

bur - den of my heart rolled a - way; it was there by faith I re -

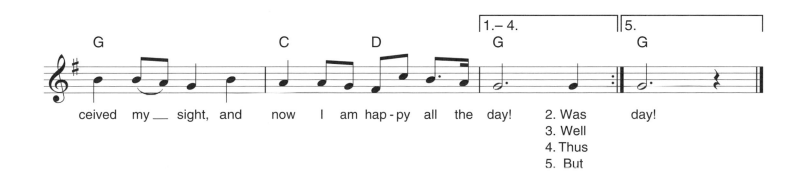

ceived my __ sight, and now I am hap - py all the day! 2. Was   day!
3. Well
4. Thus
5. But

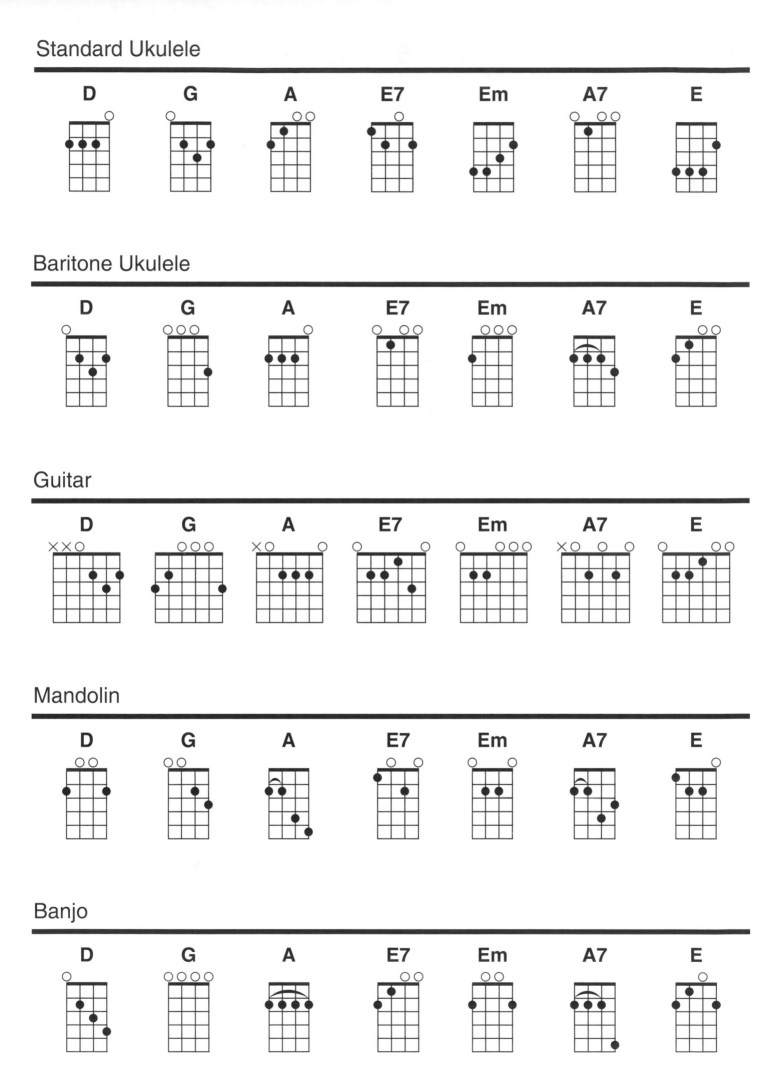

Blessed Assurance

Lyrics by Fanny J. Crosby
Music by Phoebe Palmer Knapp

Standard Ukulele

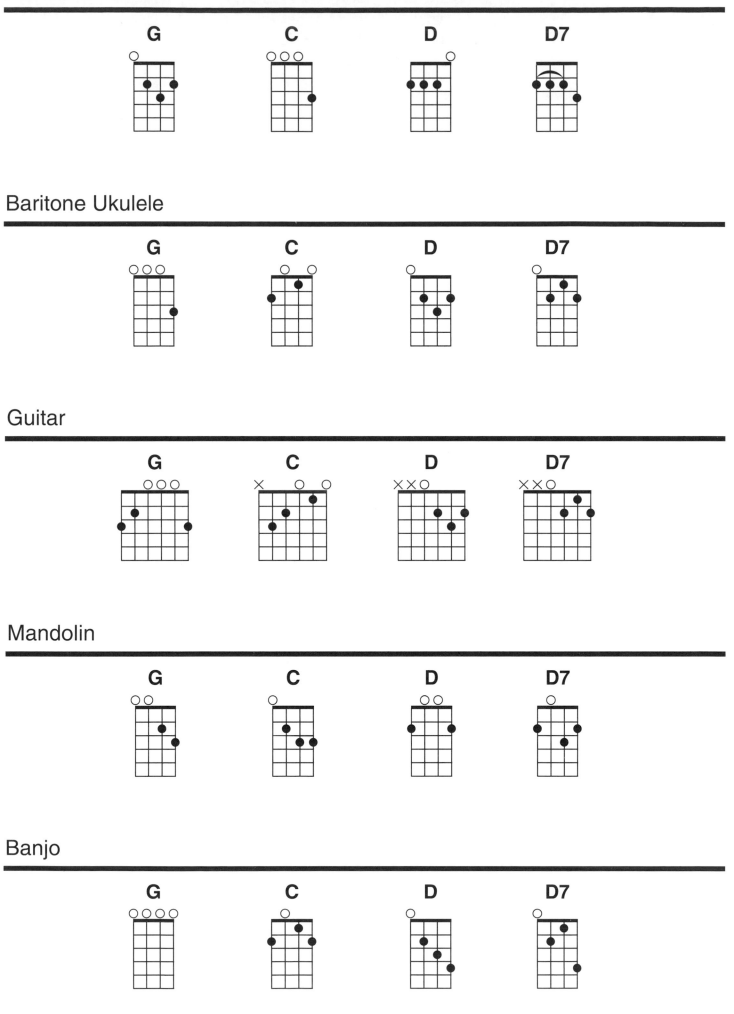

Baritone Ukulele

Guitar

Mandolin

Banjo

Blessed Be the Name

Words by Charles Wesley and Ralph E. Hudson
Traditional

Standard Ukulele

D　**F°7**　**A7**　**G**

Baritone Ukulele

D　**F°7**　**A7**　**G**

Guitar

D　**F°7**　**A7**　**G**

Mandolin

D　**F°7**　**A7**　**G**

Banjo

D　**F°7**　**A7**　**G**

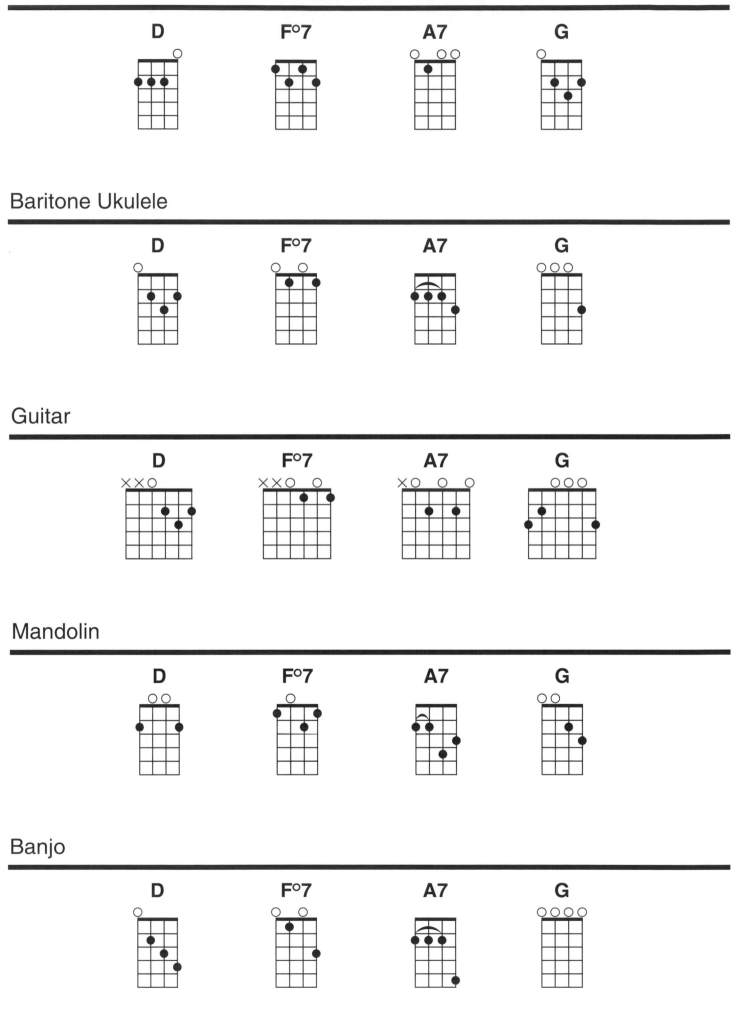

Brighten the Corner Where You Are

Words by Ina Duley Ogdon
Music by Charles H. Gabriel

Standard Ukulele

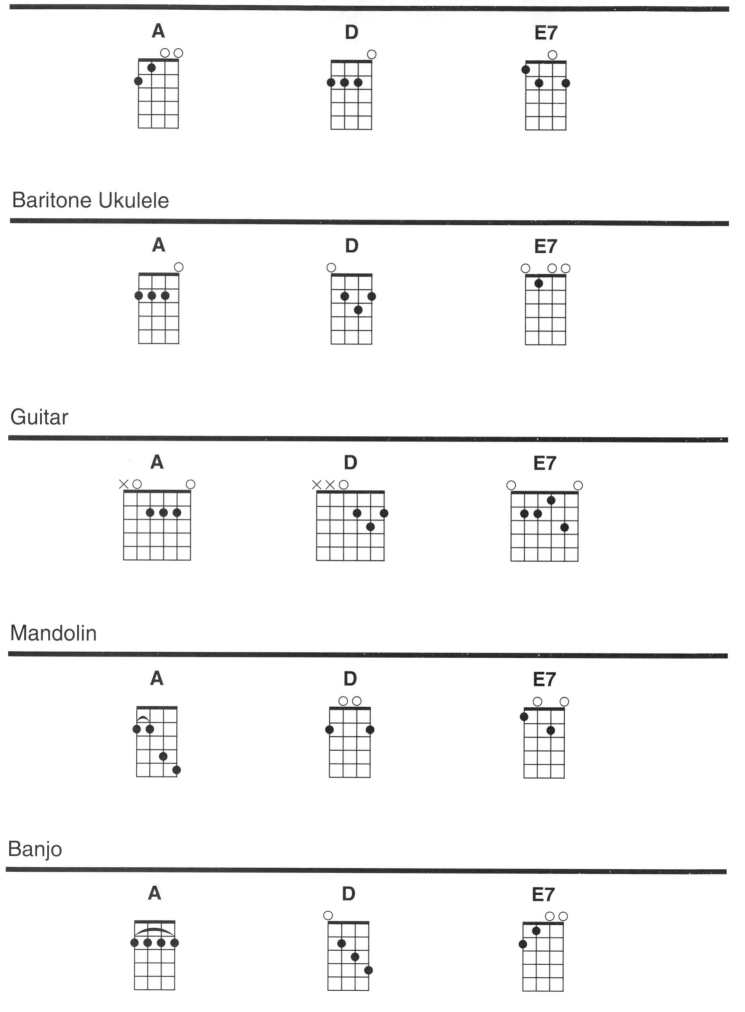

Baritone Ukulele

Guitar

Mandolin

Banjo

Church in the Wildwood

Words and Music by Dr. William S. Pitts

Standard Ukulele

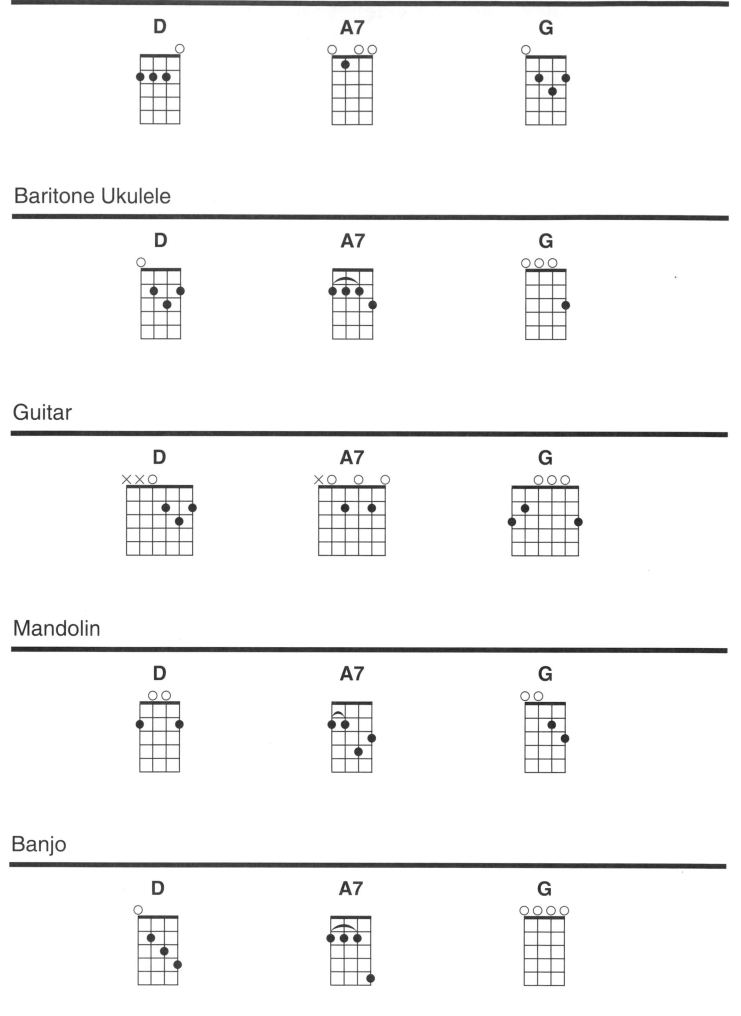

Baritone Ukulele

Guitar

Mandolin

Banjo

Count Your Blessings

Words by Johnson Oatman, Jr.
Music by Edwin O. Excell

Standard Ukulele

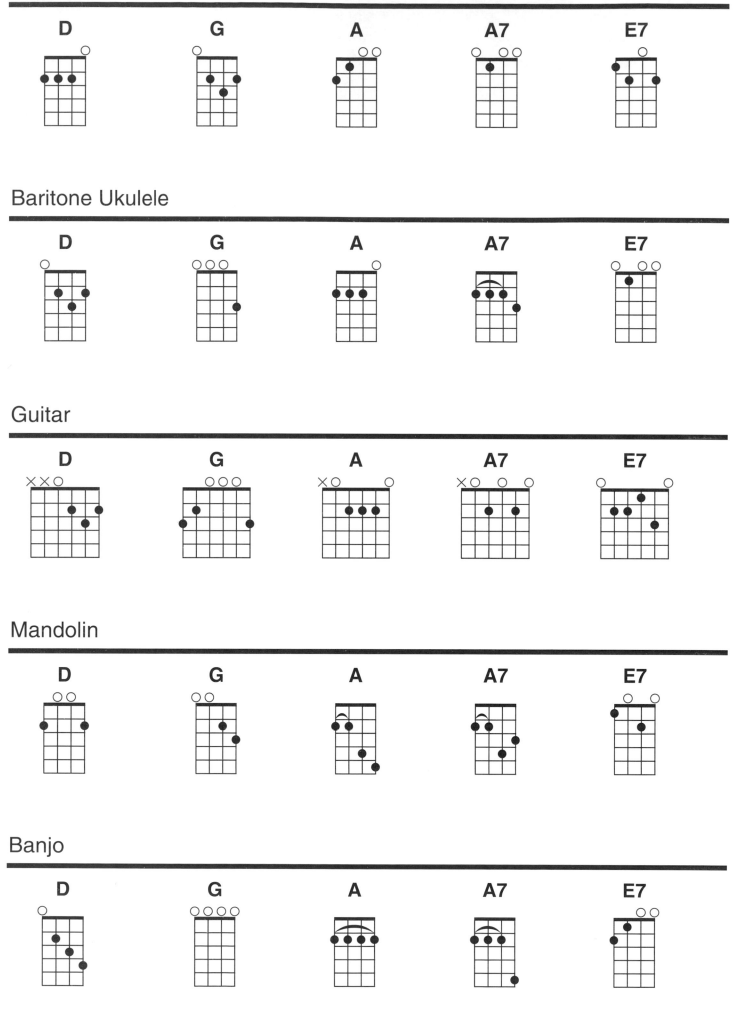

| D | G | A | A7 | E7 |

Baritone Ukulele

| D | G | A | A7 | E7 |

Guitar

| D | G | A | A7 | E7 |

Mandolin

| D | G | A | A7 | E7 |

Banjo

| D | G | A | A7 | E7 |

Does Jesus Care?

Words by Frank E. Graeff
Music by J. Lincoln Hall

Standard Ukulele

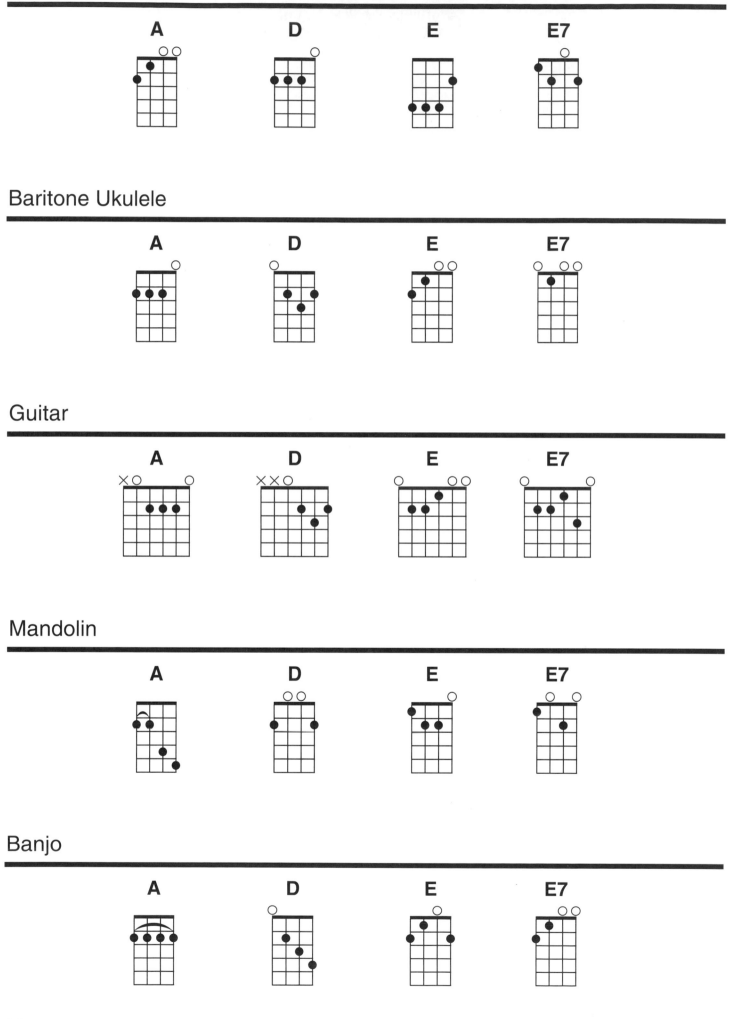

Baritone Ukulele

Guitar

Mandolin

Banjo

Down at the Cross
(Glory to His Name)

Words by Elisha A. Hoffman
Music by John H. Stockton

Standard Ukulele

G	D7	G7	C	Am7

Baritone Ukulele

G	D7	G7	C	Am7

Guitar

G	D7	G7	C	Am7

Mandolin

G	D7	G7	C	Am7

Banjo

G	D7	G7	C	Am7

Down By the Riverside

African American Spiritual

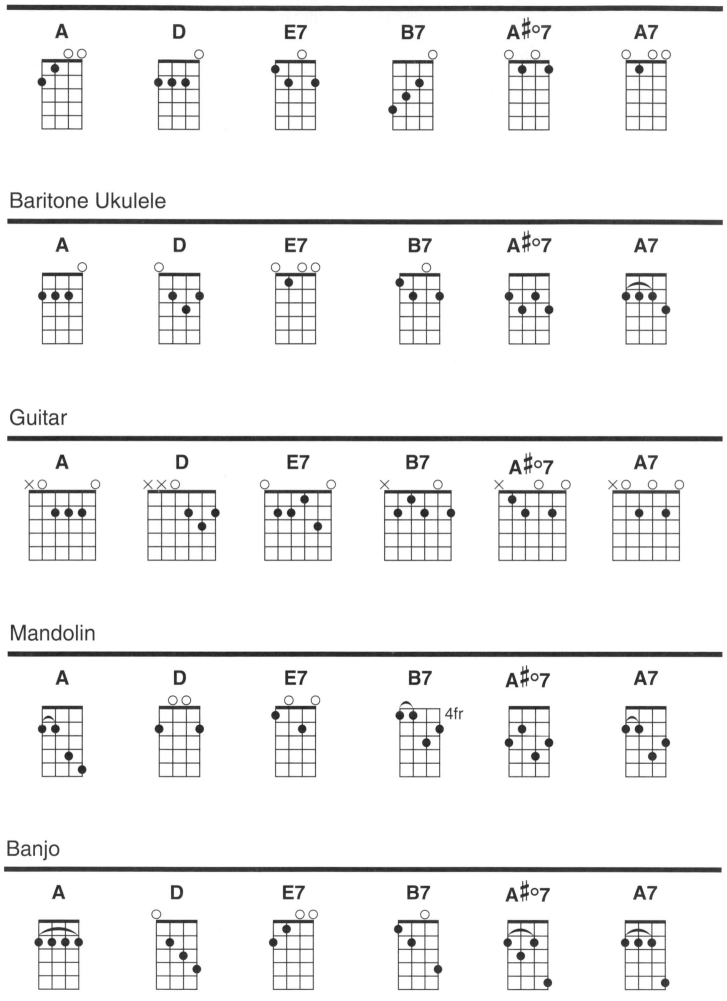

Dwelling in Beulah Land

African American Spiritual

Standard Ukulele

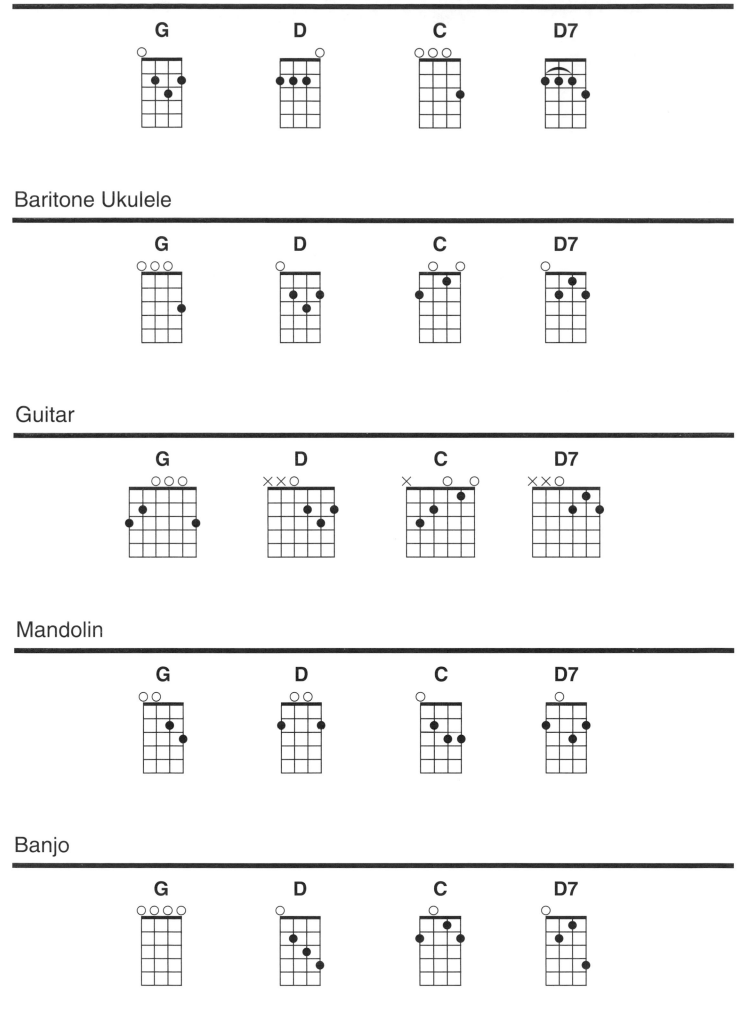

Baritone Ukulele

Guitar

Mandolin

Banjo

The Eastern Gate

Words and Music by Isaiah G. Martin

Standard Ukulele

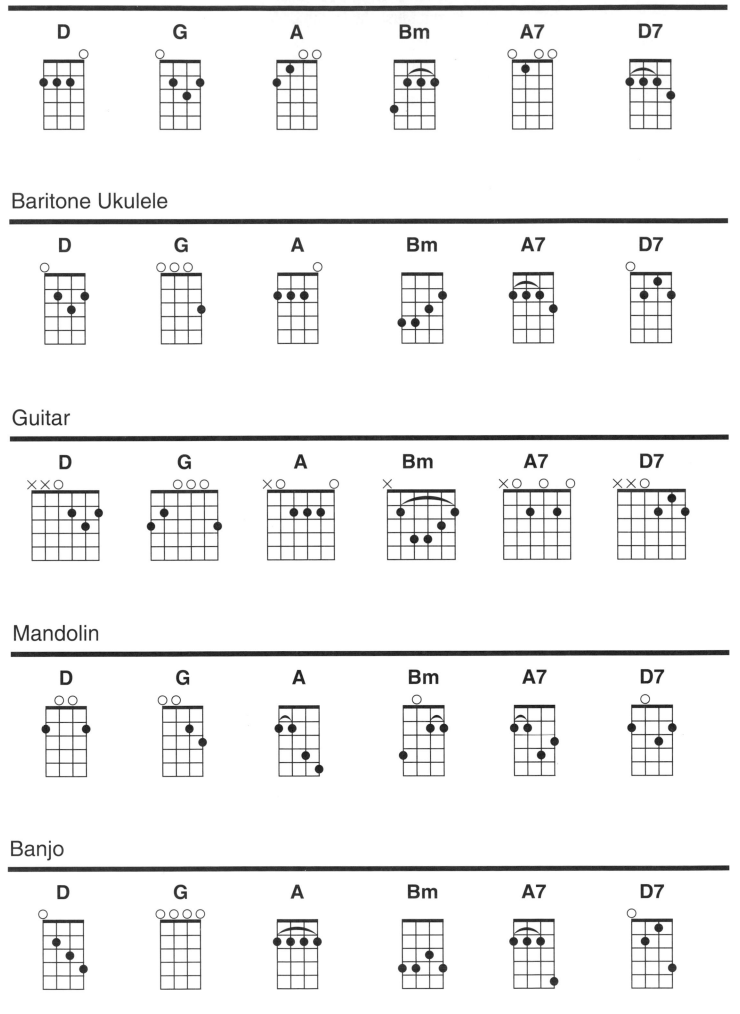

Baritone Ukulele

Guitar

Mandolin

Banjo

Footsteps of Jesus

Words by Mary B.C. Slade
Music by Asa B. Everett

Verse
Moderately fast

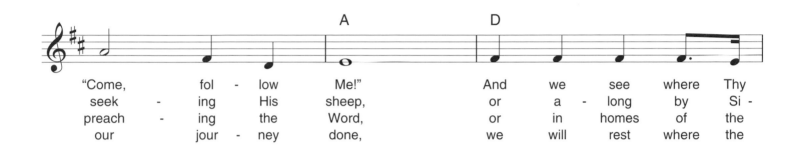

1. Sweet - ly, Lord, have we heard Thee call - ing,
2. Though they lead o'er the cold, dark moun - tains,
3. If they lead through the tem - ple ho - ly,
4. Then at last, when on high He sees us,

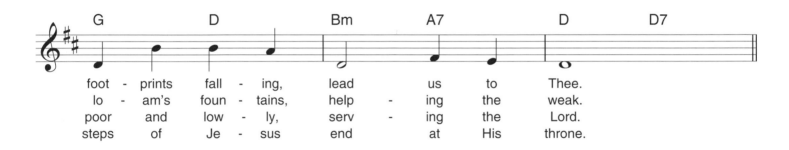

"Come, fol - low Me!" And we see where Thy
seek - ing His sheep, or a - long by Si -
preach - ing the Word, or in homes of the
our jour - ney done, we will rest where the

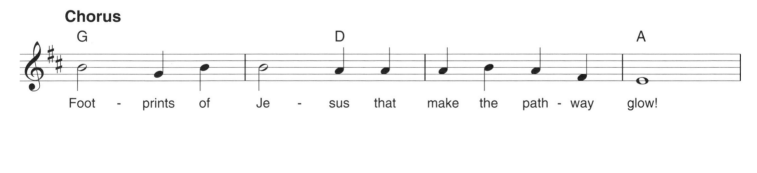

foot - prints fall - ing, lead us to Thee.
lo - am's foun - tains, help - ing the weak.
poor and low - ly, serv - ing the Lord.
steps of Je - sus end at His throne.

Chorus

Foot - prints of Je - sus that make the path - way glow!

Play 4 times

We will fol - low the steps of Je - sus wher - e'er they go.

Standard Ukulele

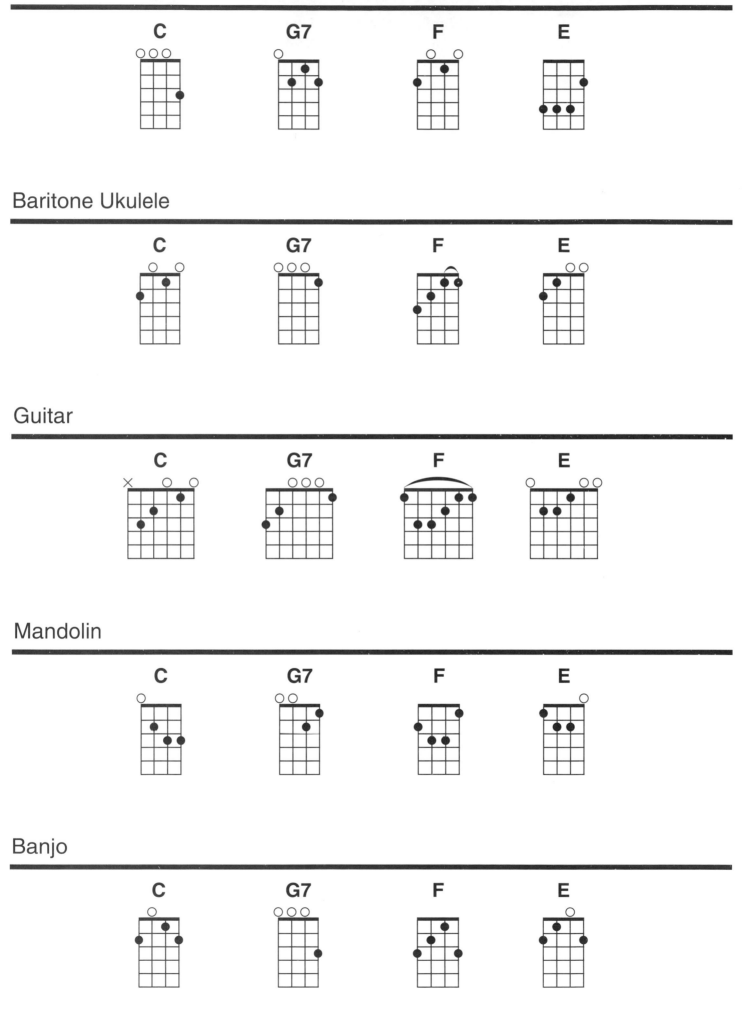

Baritone Ukulele

Guitar

Mandolin

Banjo

God Will Take Care of You

Words by Civilla D. Martin
Music by W. Stillman Martin

Verse
Moderately

1. Be not dis - mayed ___ what - e'er be - tide;
2. Through days of toil ___ when heart doth fail,
3. All you may need ___ He will pro - vide;
4. No mat - ter what ___ may be the test,

God will take care of you. ___

Be - neath His wings ___ of love a - bide;
When dan - gers fierce ___ your path as - sail,
Noth - ing you ask ___ will be de - nied;
Lean, wea - ry one, ___ up - on His breast;

God will take care of you. ___

Chorus

God will take care of you, through ev - 'ry
day, o'er all the way. He will take
care ___ of you. God will take care ___ of you. ___

Play 4 times

Standard Ukulele

D G A7 E7 A D°7 B Em

Baritone Ukulele

D G A7 E7 A D°7 B7 Em

Guitar

D G A7 E7 A D°7 B7 Em

Mandolin

D G A7 E7 A D°7 B7 Em

Banjo

D G A7 E7 A D°7 B7 Em

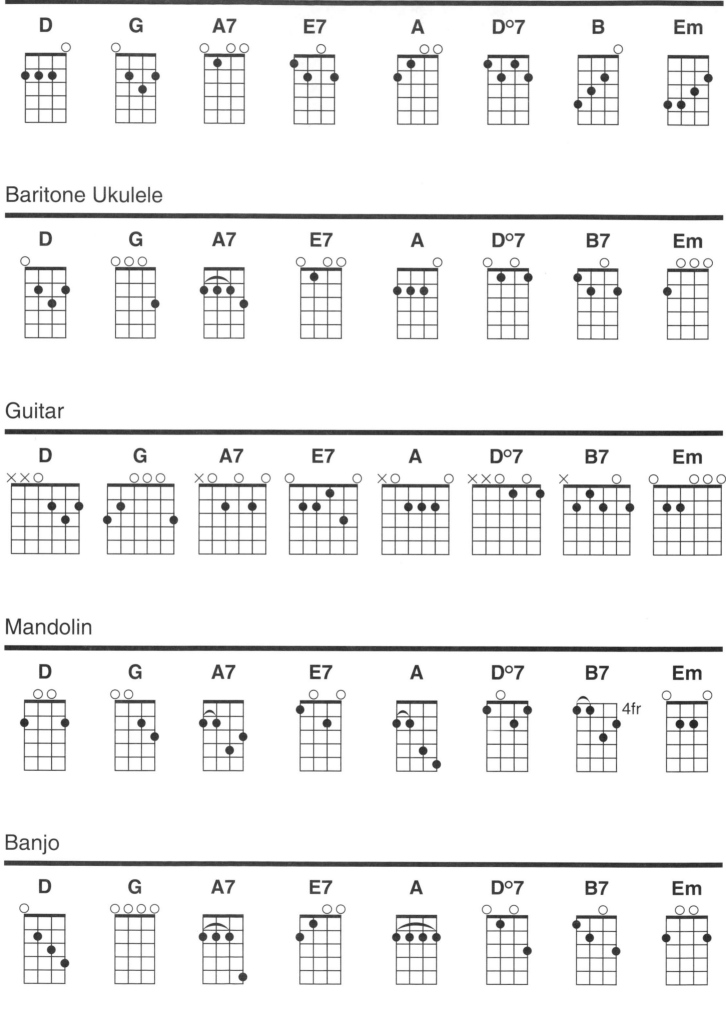

Great Is Thy Faithfulness

Words by Thomas O. Chisholm
Music by William M. Runyan

Verse
Moderately

| D | G | A7 | D |

1. Great is Thy faith - ful - ness, O God, my Fa - ther.
2. Sum - mer and win - ter and spring - time and har - vest;
3. Par - don for sin and a peace that en - dur - eth,

| G | D | E7 | A |

There is no shad - ow of turn - ing with Thee.
sun, moon and stars in their cours - es a - bove
Thine own dear pres - ence to cheer and to guide,

| A7 | D | G |

Thou chang - est not, Thy com - pas - sions, they fail not.
join with all na - ture in man - i - fold wit - ness
strength for to - day and bright hope for to - mor - row,

| D°7 | D | A7 | D |

As Thou hast been, Thou for - ev - er wilt be.
to Thy great faith - ful - ness, mer - cy and love.
bless - ings all mine, with ten thou - sand be - side.

Chorus

| A | D | B7 | Em |

Great is Thy faith - ful - ness! Great is Thy faith - ful - ness!

| A7 | D | A | E7 | A |

Morn - ing by morn - ing new mer - cies I see.

| A7 | D | G | D | G |

All I have need - ed Thy hand hath pro - vid - ed.

| D°7 | D | Em | A7 | D | *Play 3 times* |

Great is Thy faith - ful - ness, Lord, un - to me!

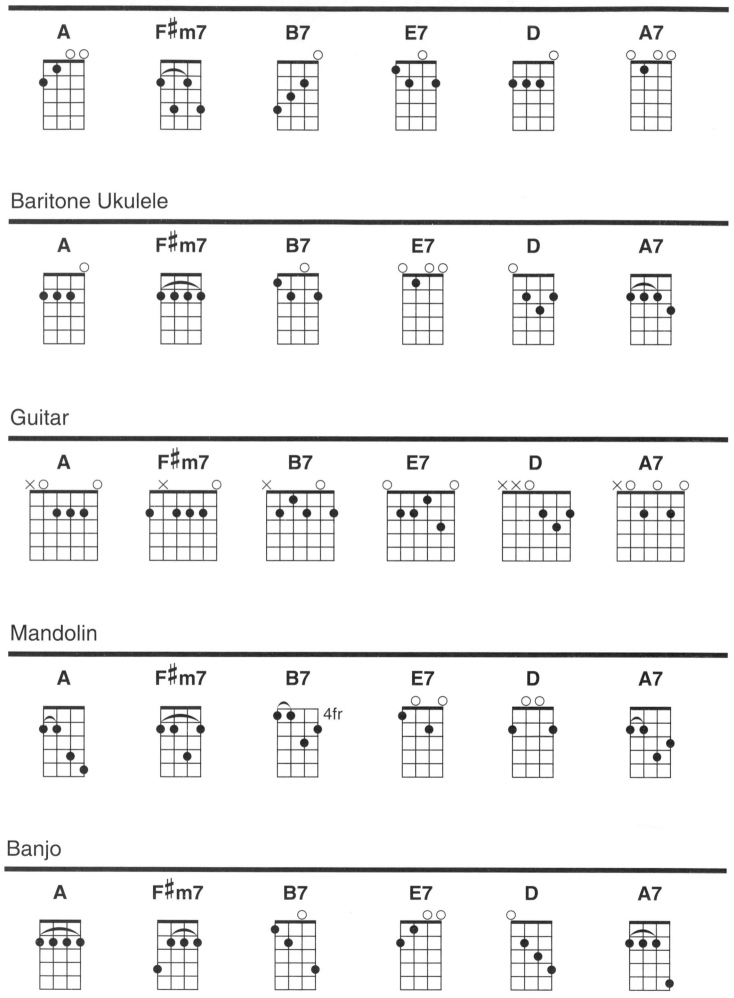

Hallelujah, We Shall Rise

By J.E. Thomas

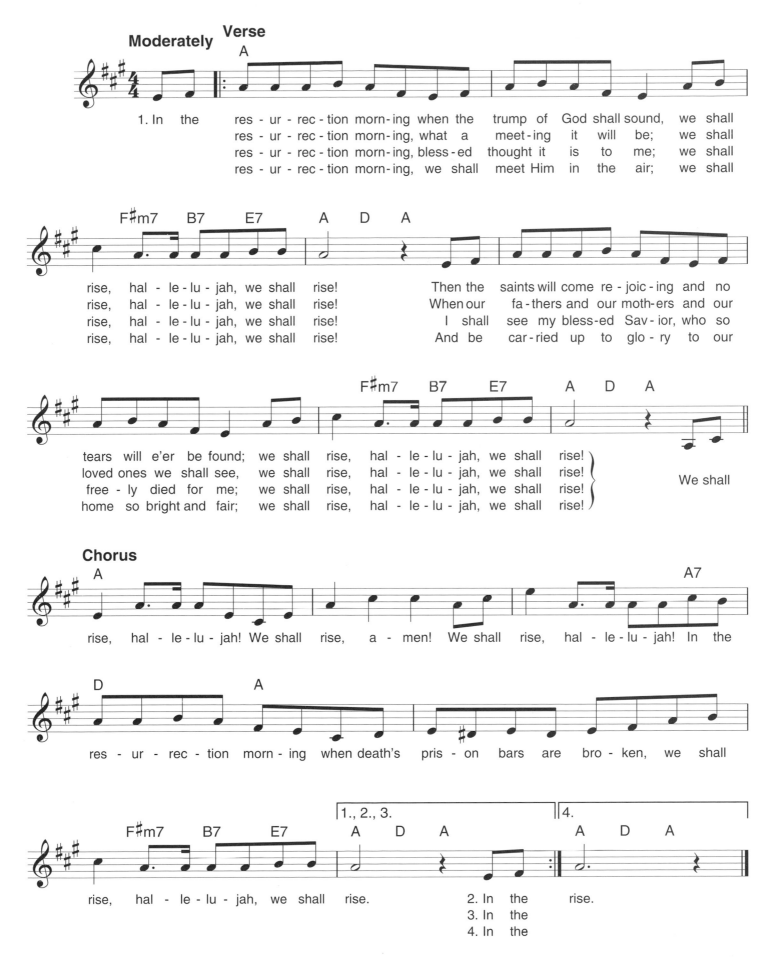

Standard Ukulele

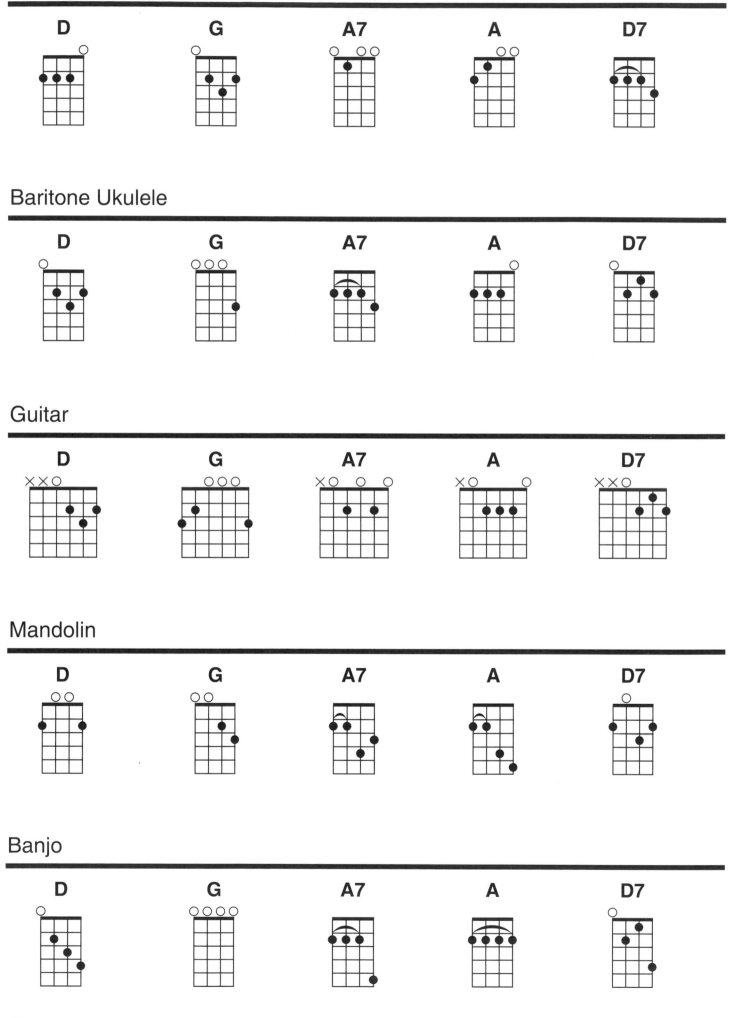

Baritone Ukulele

Guitar

Mandolin

Banjo

He Hideth My Soul

Words by Fanny J. Crosby
Music by William J. Kirkpatrick

Standard Ukulele

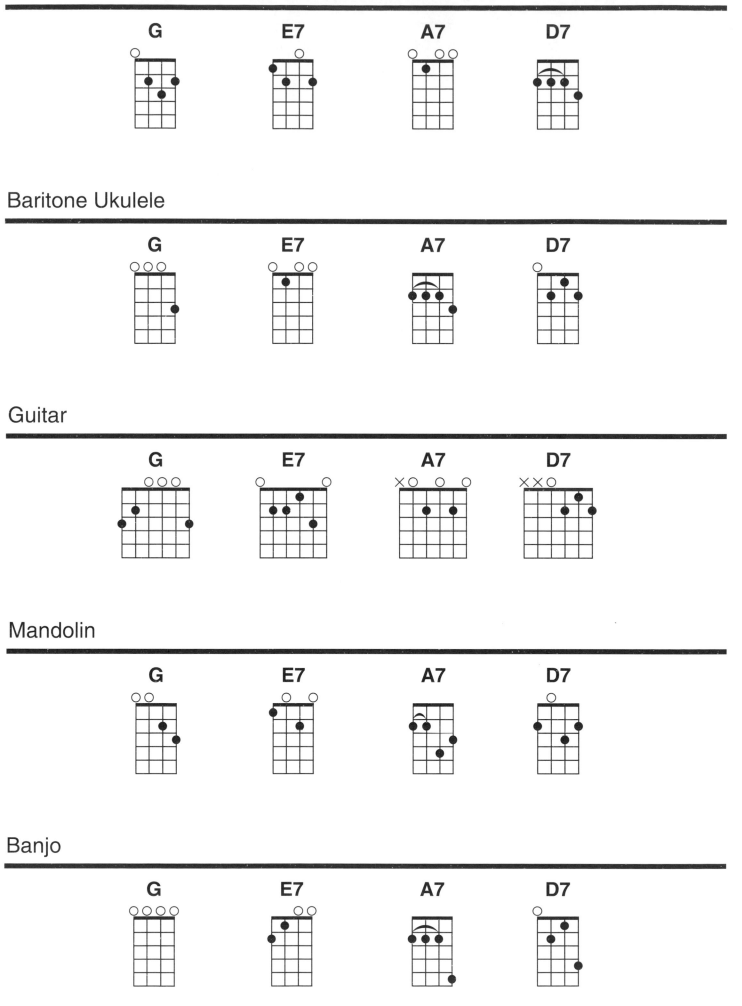

Baritone Ukulele

Guitar

Mandolin

Banjo

He Keeps Me Singing

Words and Music by Luther B. Bridgers

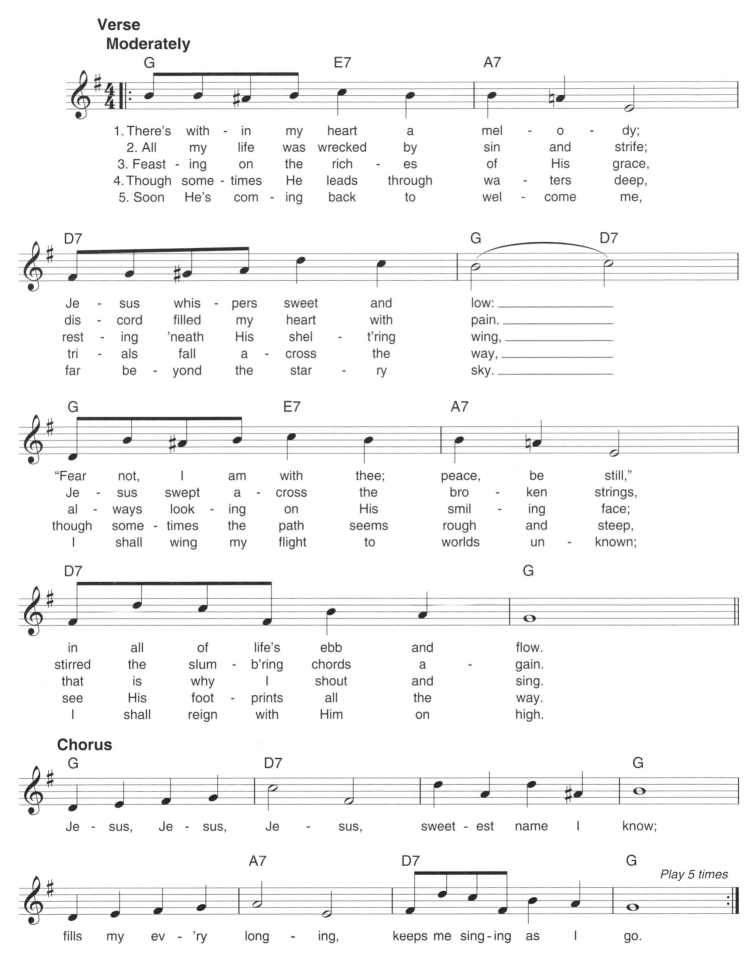

Standard Ukulele

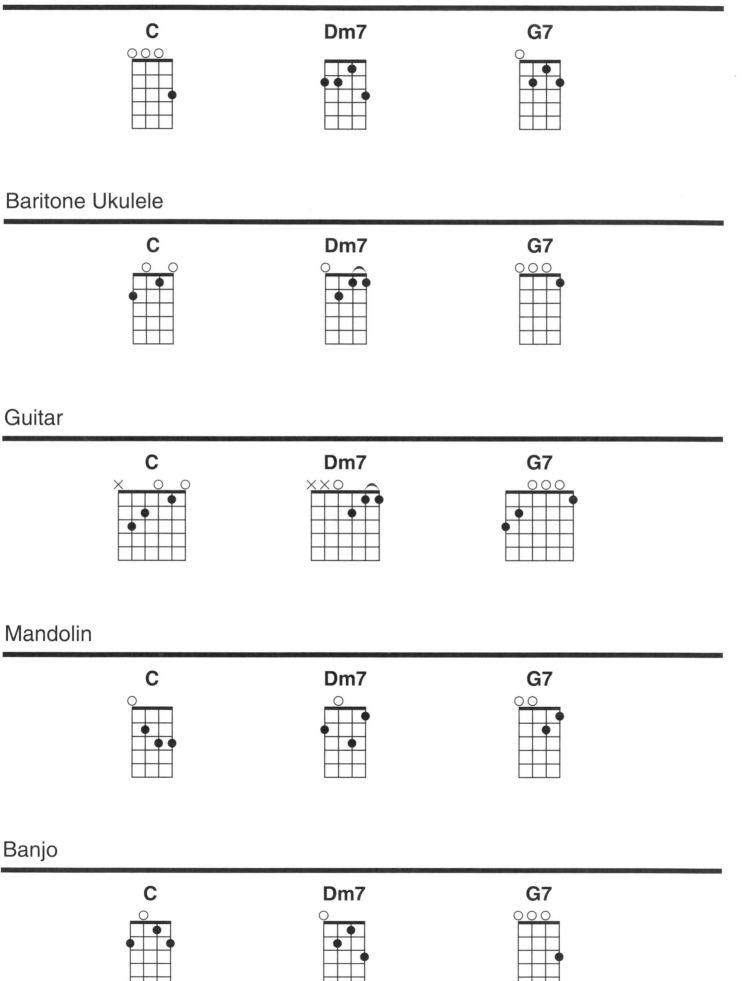

Baritone Ukulele

Guitar

Mandolin

Banjo

He's Got the Whole World in His Hands

Traditional Spiritual

Standard Ukulele

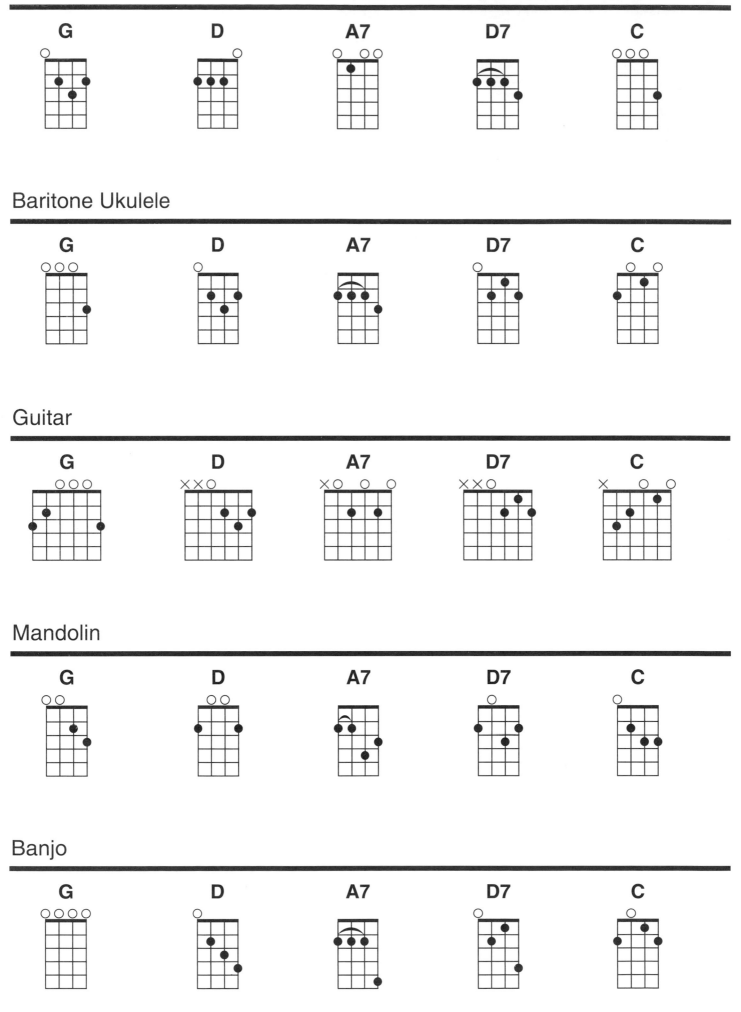

Baritone Ukulele

Guitar

Mandolin

Banjo

Heavenly Sunlight

Words by Henry J. Zelley
Music by George Harrison Cook

Standard Ukulele

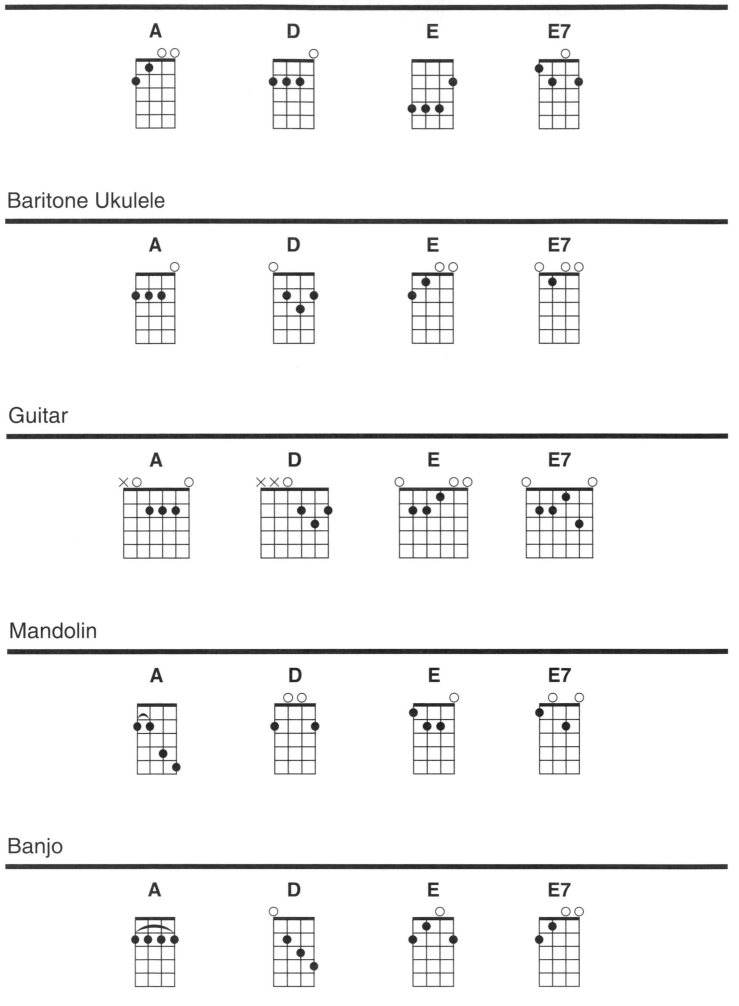

Baritone Ukulele

Guitar

Mandolin

Banjo

Higher Ground

Words by Johnson Oatman, Jr.
Music by Charles H. Gabriel

Standard Ukulele

C F A7 Dm Fm G7 C#°7 C7

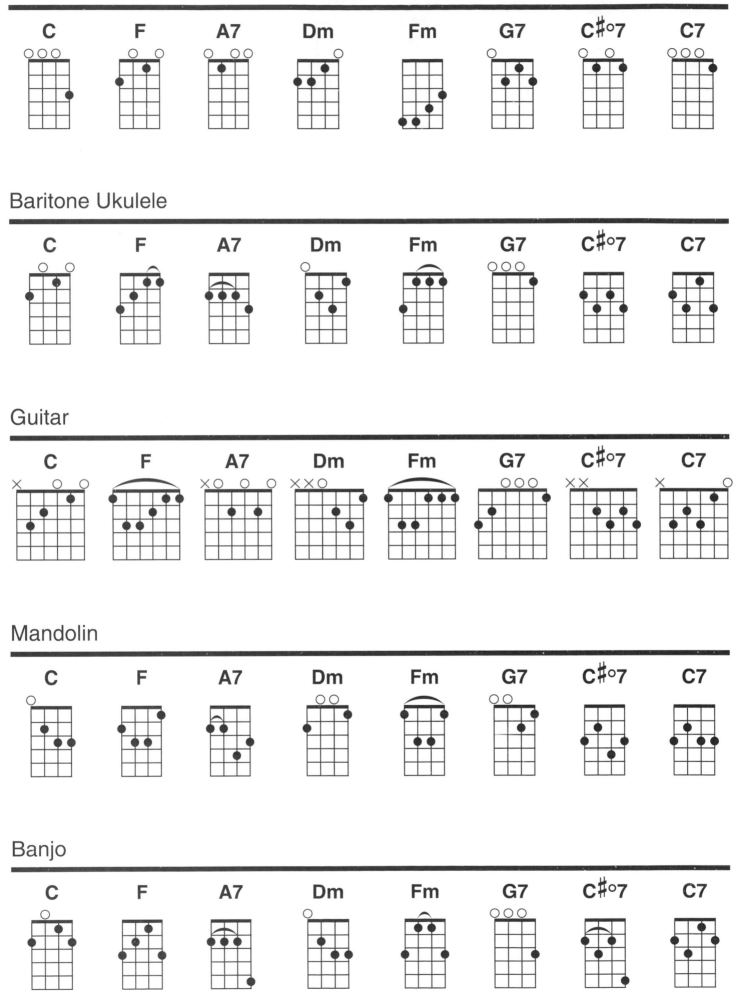

Baritone Ukulele

C F A7 Dm Fm G7 C#°7 C7

Guitar

C F A7 Dm Fm G7 C#°7 C7

Mandolin

C F A7 Dm Fm G7 C#°7 C7

Banjo

C F A7 Dm Fm G7 C#°7 C7

His Eye Is on the Sparrow

Words by Civilla D. Martin
Music by Charles H. Gabriel

Standard Ukulele

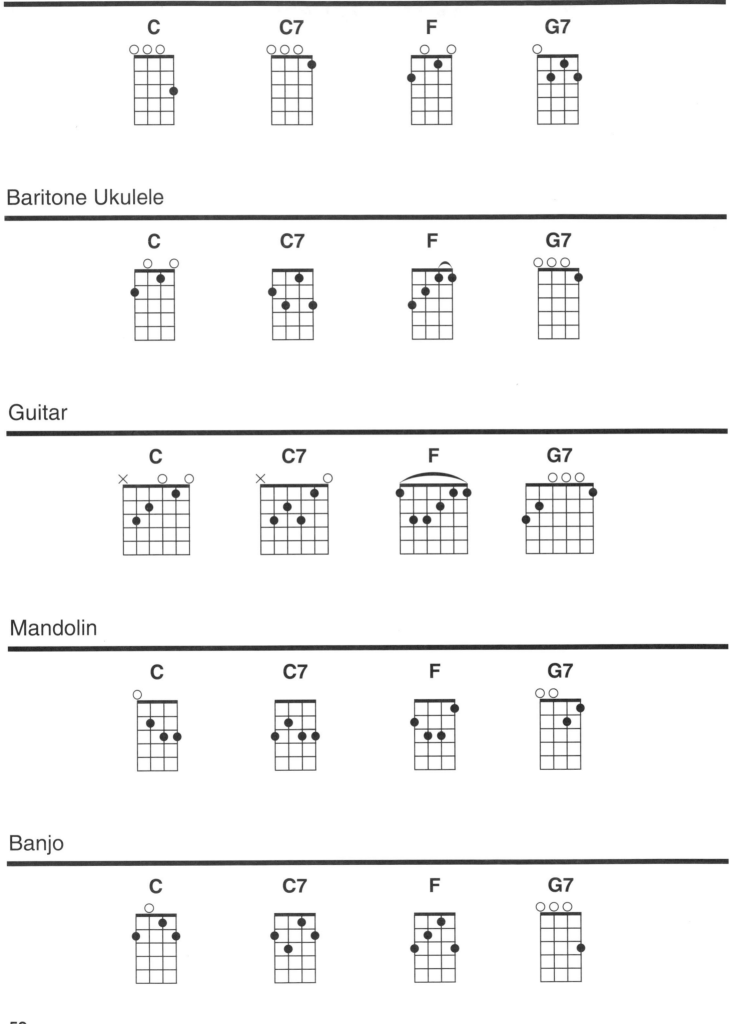

Baritone Ukulele

Guitar

Mandolin

Banjo

I Have Decided to Follow Jesus

Folk Melody from India

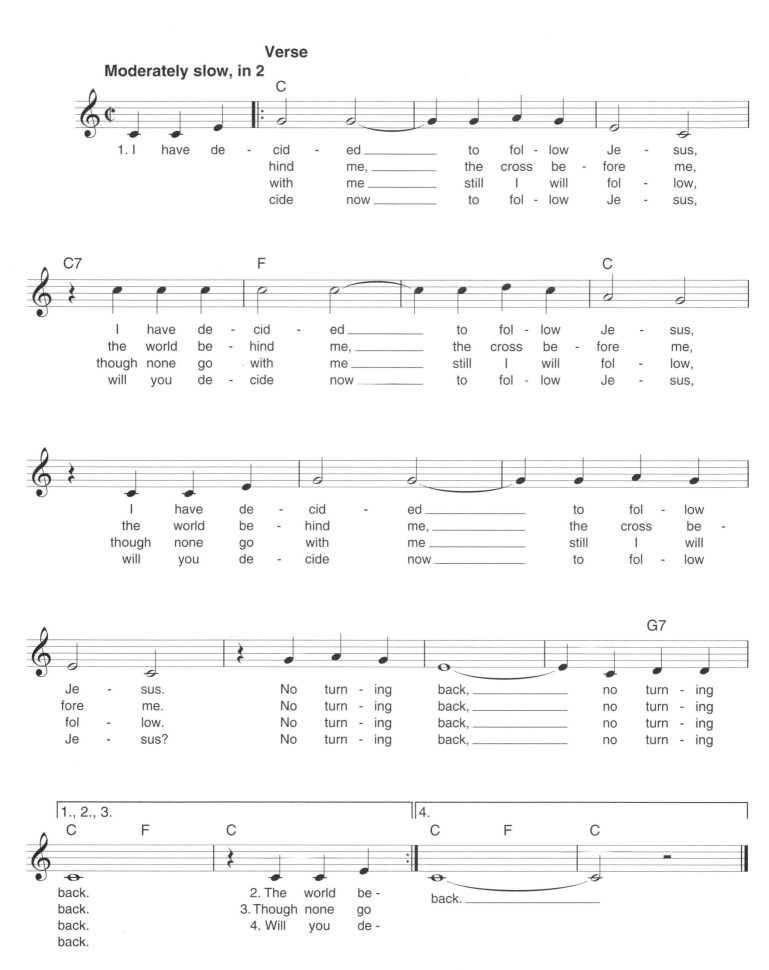

Standard Ukulele

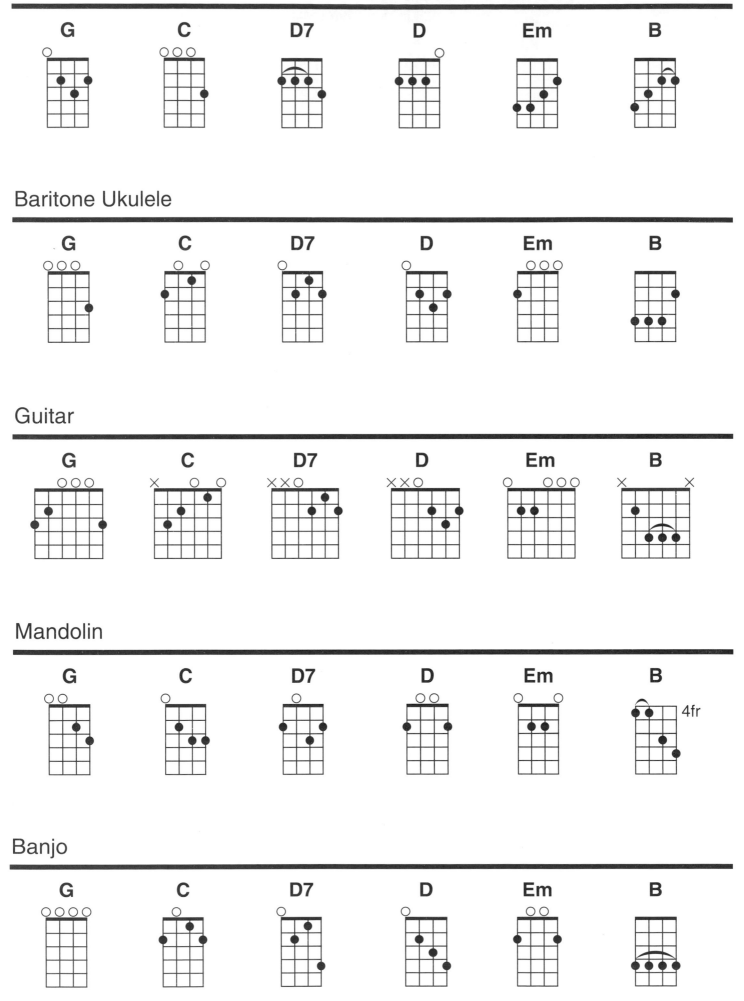

Baritone Ukulele

Guitar

Mandolin

Banjo

I Love to Tell the Story

Words by A. Catherine Hankey
Music by William G. Fischer

Standard Ukulele

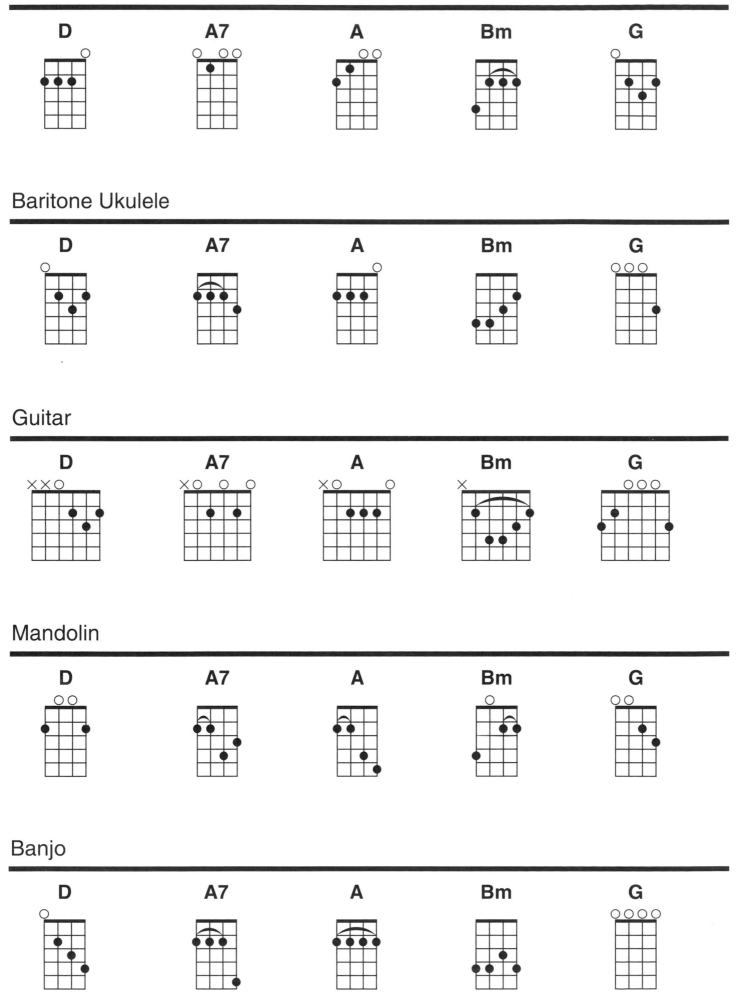

Baritone Ukulele

Guitar

Mandolin

Banjo

I Must Tell Jesus

Words and Music by Elisha A. Hoffman

Standard Ukulele

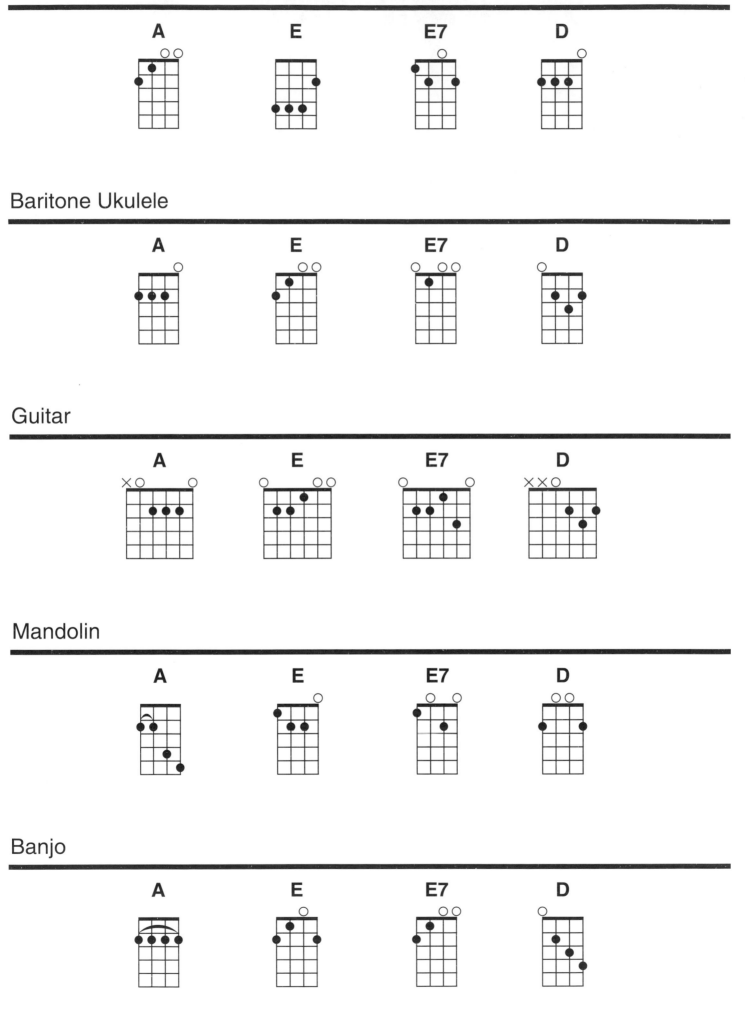

Baritone Ukulele

Guitar

Mandolin

Banjo

I Stand Amazed in the Presence
(My Savior's Love)
Words and Music by Charles H. Gabriel

Verse
Moderately fast

1. I stand a-mazed in the pres - ence of
me it was in the gar - den He
pit - y an - gels be - held Him, and
took my sins and my sor - rows, He
with the ran - somed in glo - ry His

Je - sus the Naz - a - rene, and won - der how He could
prayed, "Not My will, but Thine." He had no tears for His
came from the world of light to com - fort Him in the
made them His ver - y own. He bore the bur - den to
face I at last shall see, 'twill be my joy through the

love me, a sin - ner, con - demned, un - clean.
own griefs, but sweat - drops of blood for mine.
sor - rows He bore for my soul that night.
Cal - v'ry and suf - fered and died a - lone.
ag - es to sing of His love for me.

Chorus

How mar - vel - ous! How won - der - ful! And my song shall

ev - er be: How mar - vel - ous! How won - der - ful

is my __ Sav - ior's love for me! 2. For me!
3. In
4. He
5. When

1.– 4. | 5.

Standard Ukulele

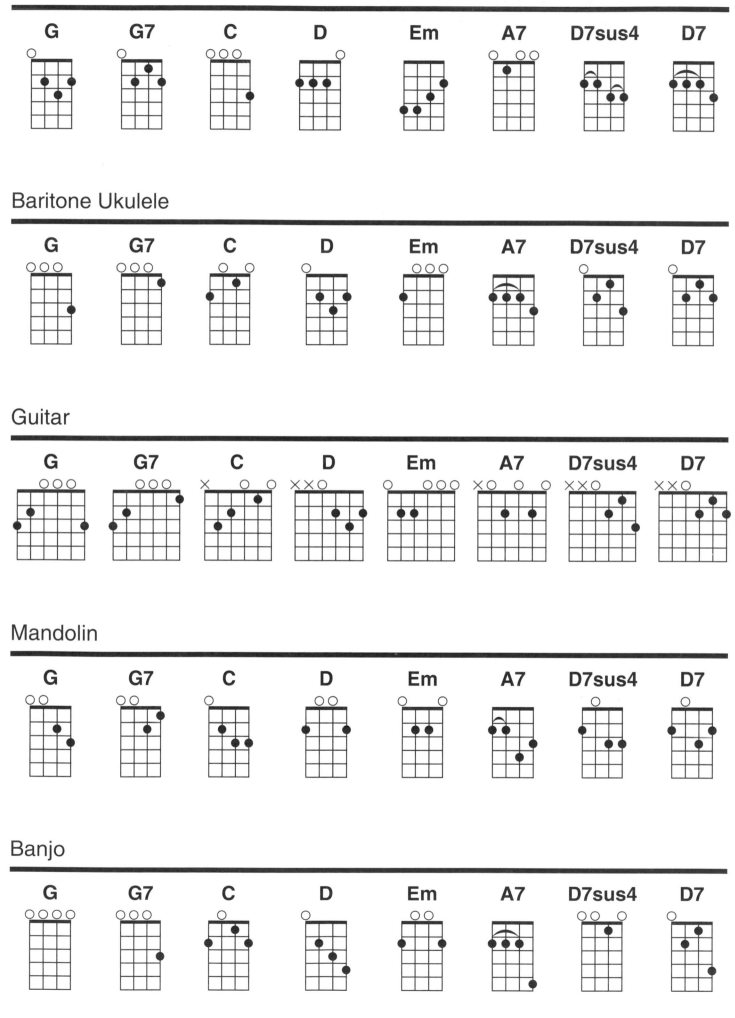

Baritone Ukulele

Guitar

Mandolin

Banjo

I've Got Peace Like a River

Traditional

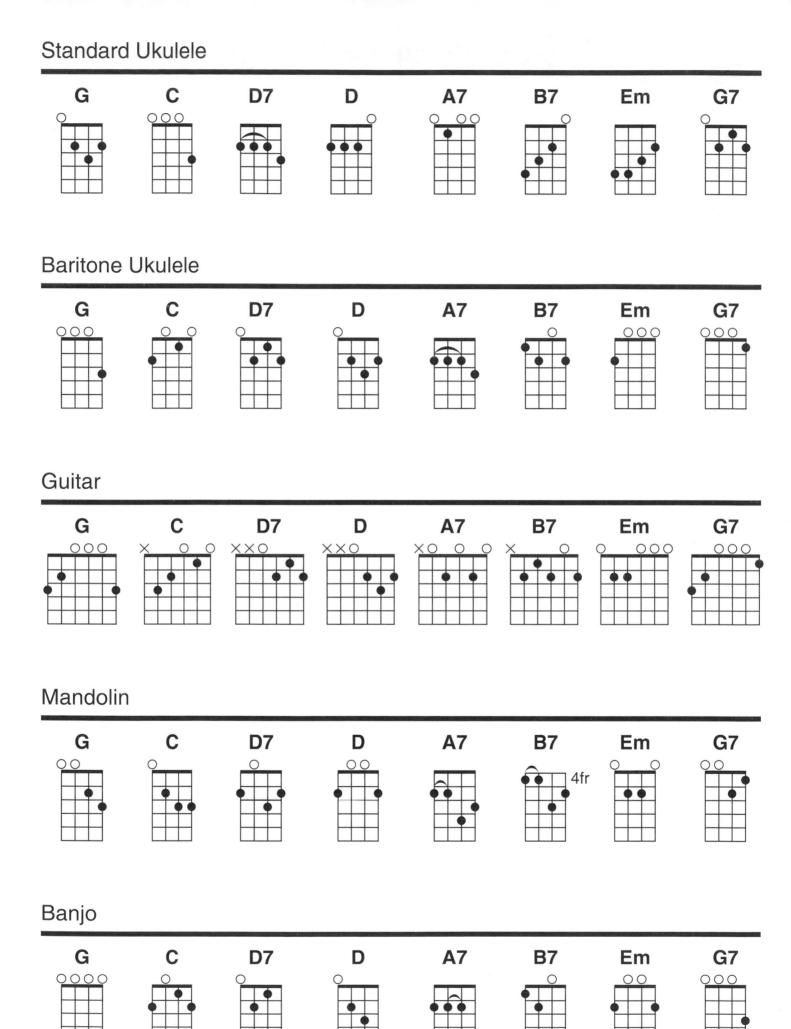

In the Garden

Words and Music by C. Austin Miles

Standard Ukulele

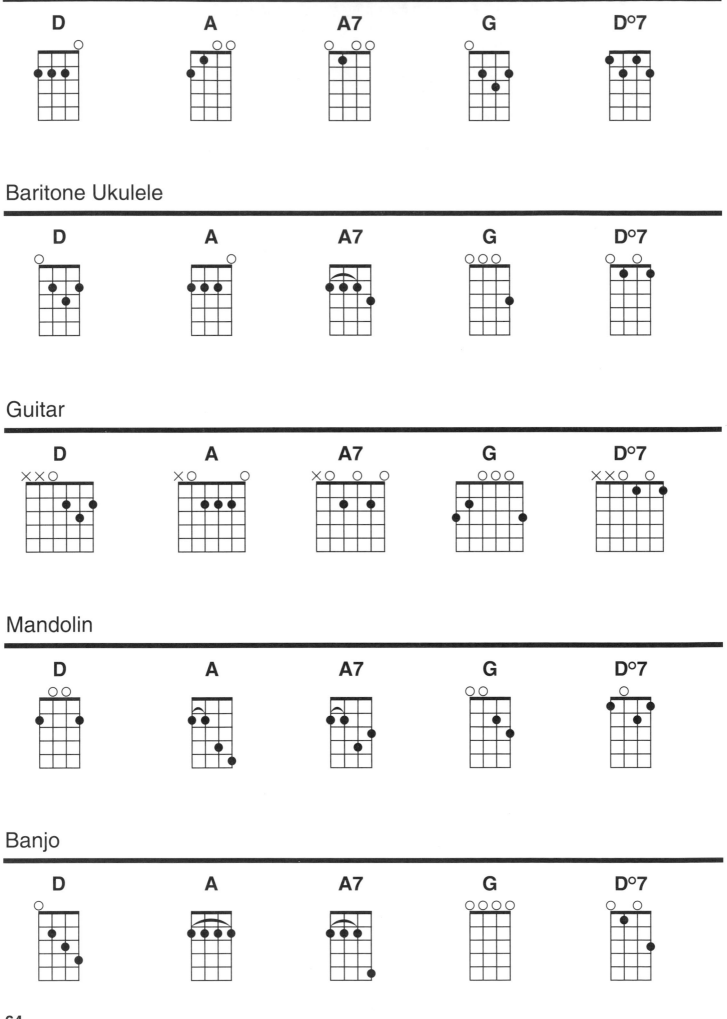

Baritone Ukulele

Guitar

Mandolin

Banjo

Jesus Paid It All

Words by Elvina M. Hall
Music by John T. Grape

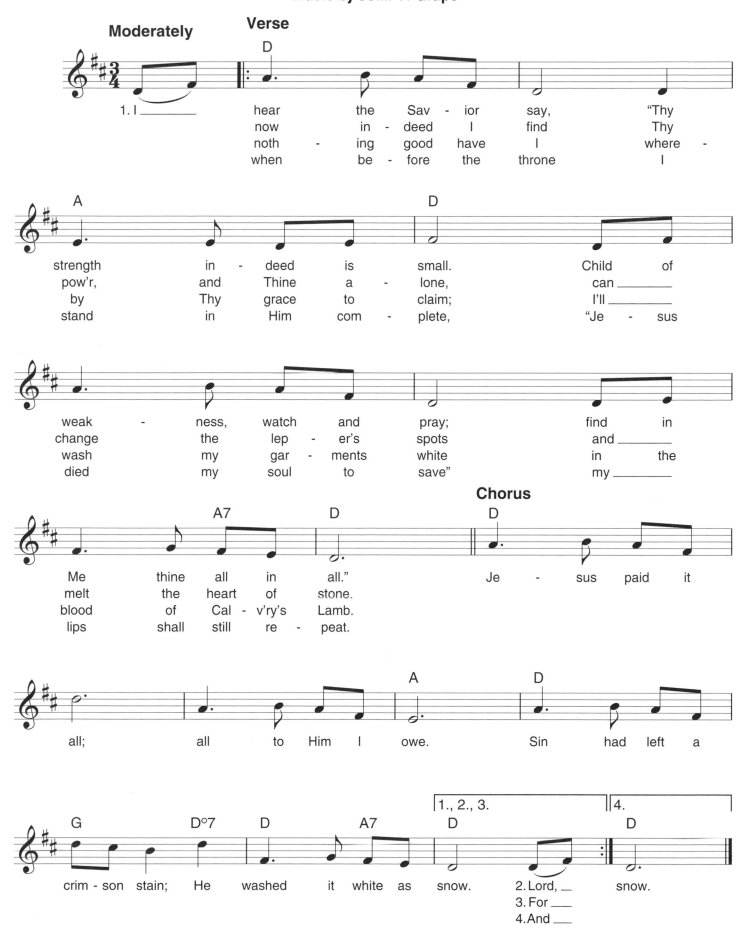

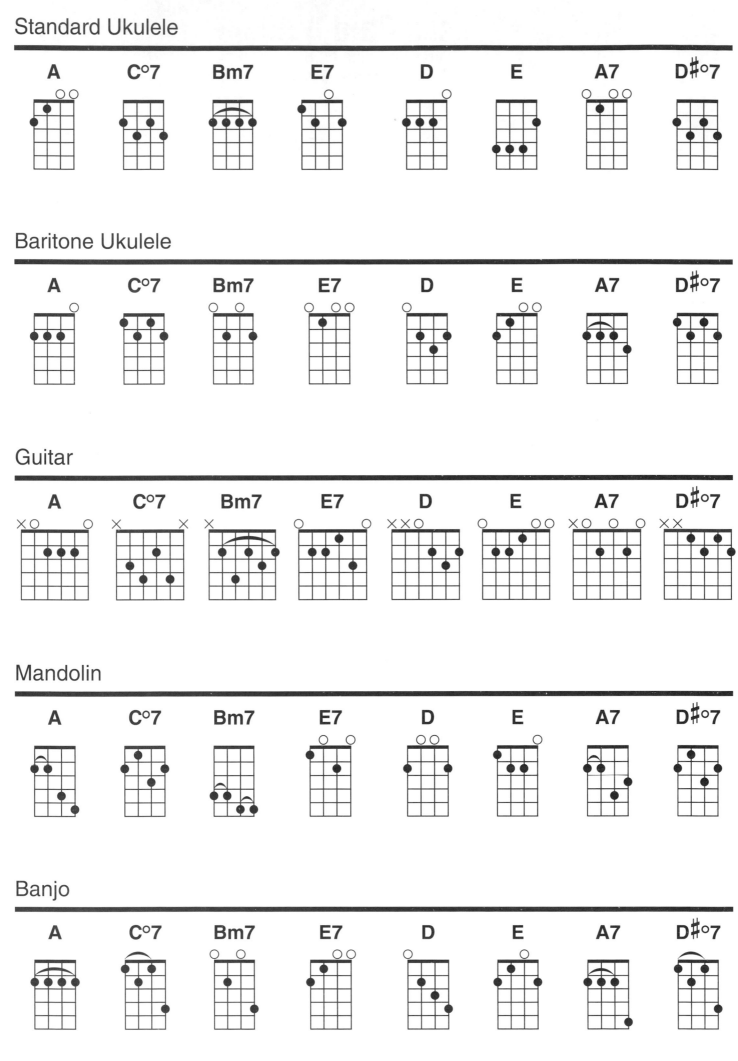

66

Just a Closer Walk with Thee

Traditional
Arranged by Kenneth Morris

Standard Ukulele

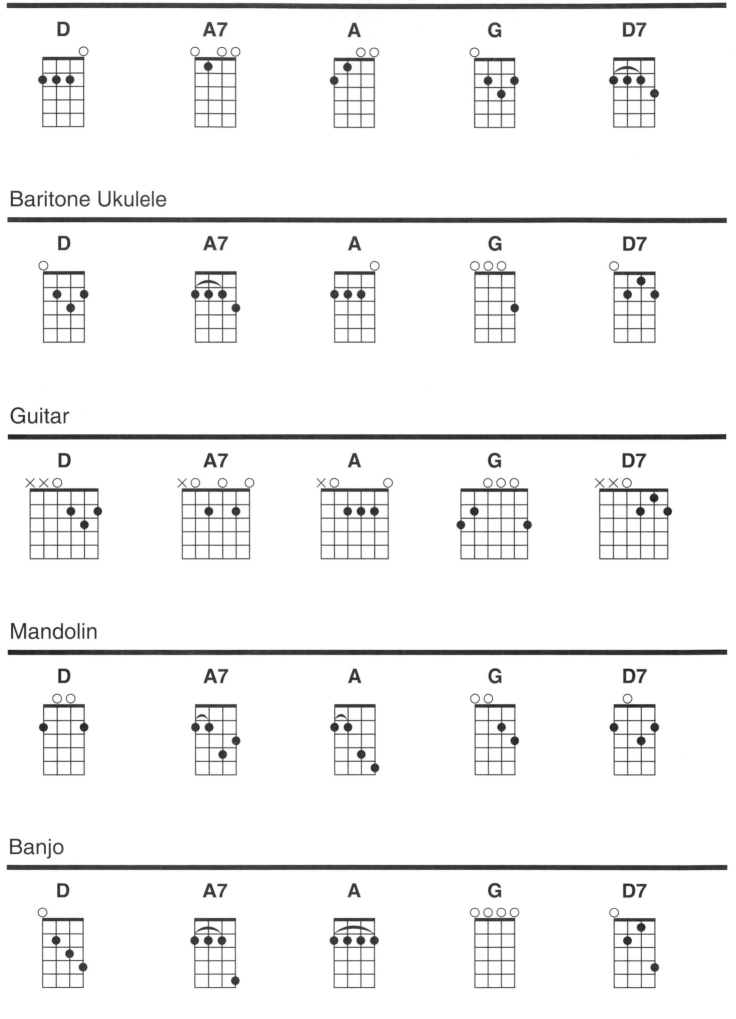

Baritone Ukulele

Guitar

Mandolin

Banjo

Just As I Am

Words by Charlotte Elliott
Music by William B. Bradbury

Standard Ukulele

Baritone Ukulele

Guitar

Mandolin

Banjo

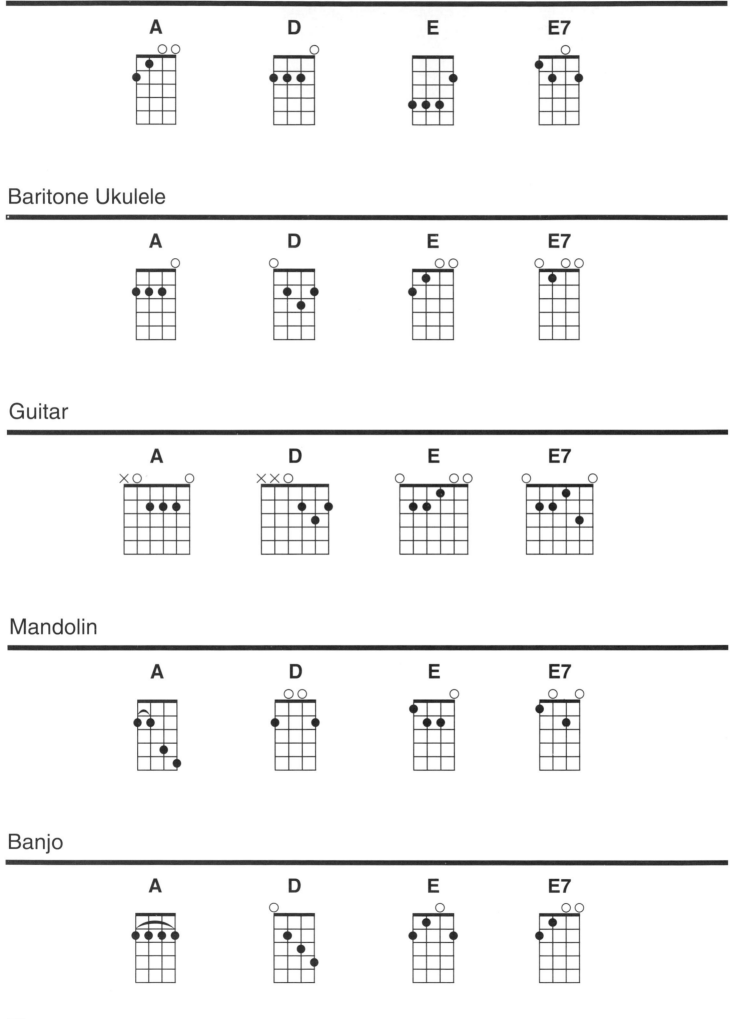

Leaning on the Everlasting Arms

Words by Elisha A. Hoffman
Music by Anthony J. Showalter

Standard Ukulele

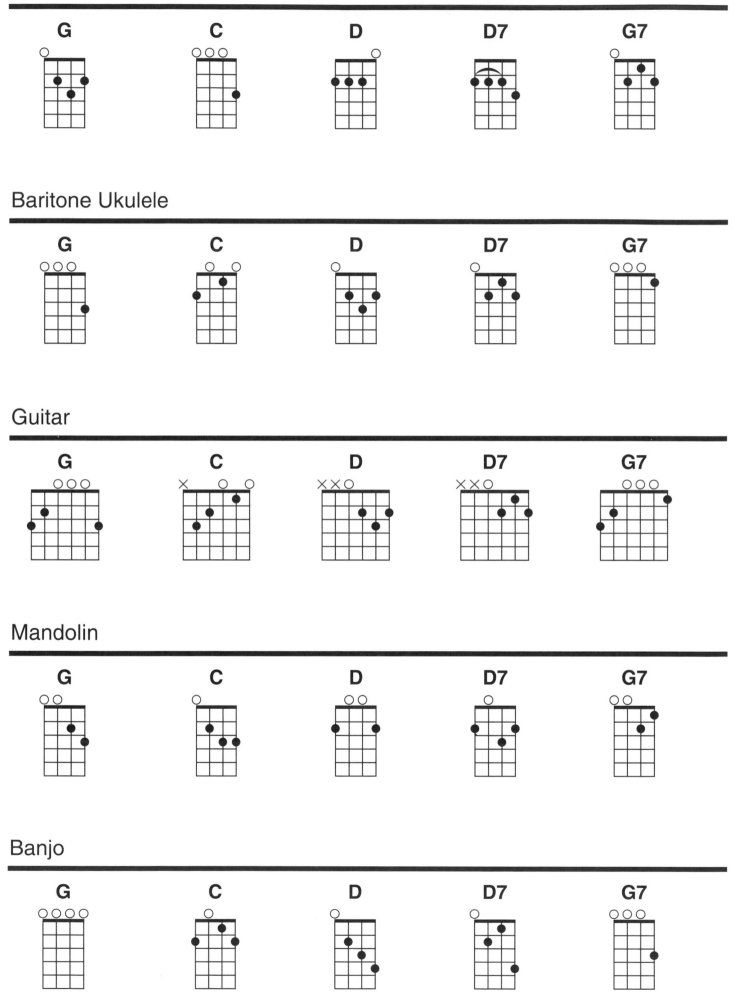

Baritone Ukulele

Guitar

Mandolin

Banjo

The Lily of the Valley

Words by Charles W. Fry
Music by William S. Hays

Standard Ukulele

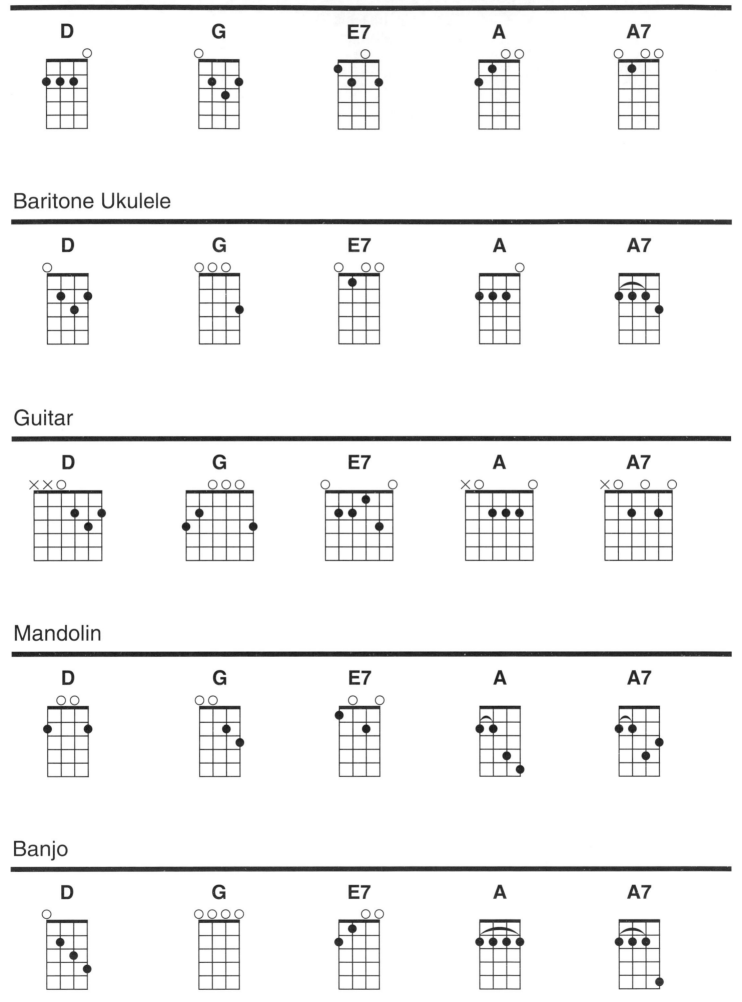

Baritone Ukulele

Guitar

Mandolin

Banjo

Little Is Much When God Is in It

Words by Mrs. F.W. Suffield and Dwight Brock
Music by Mrs. F.W. Suffield

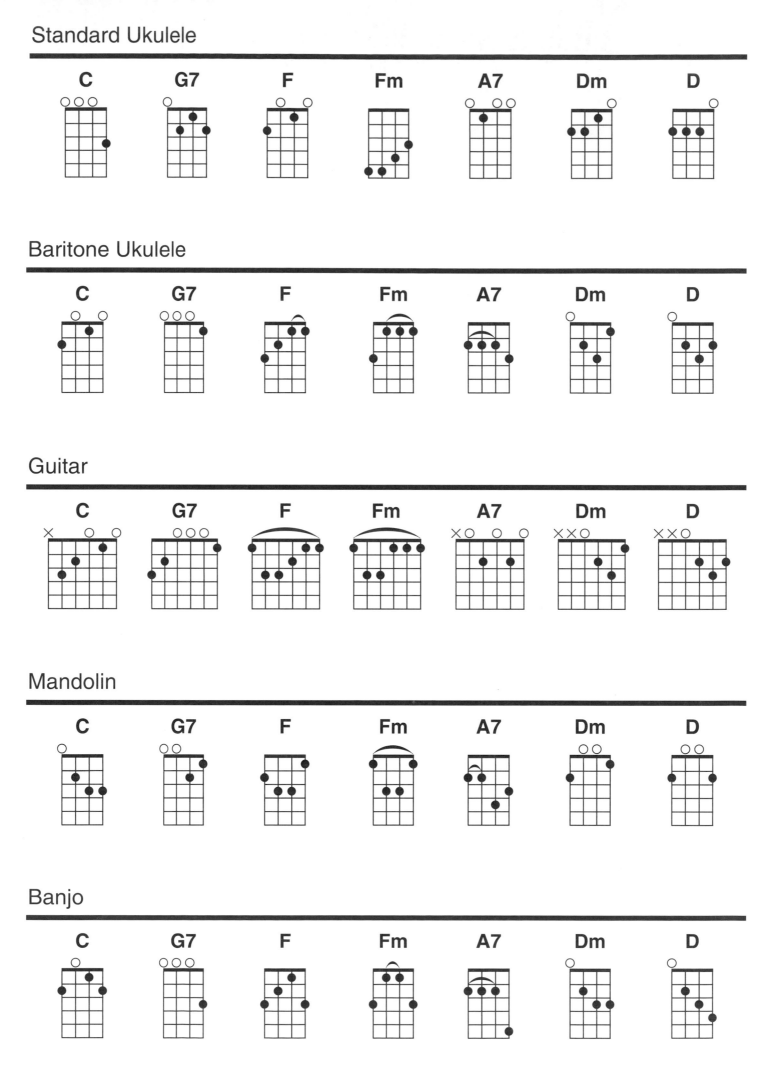

Love Lifted Me

Words by James Rowe
Music by Howard E. Smith

Verse
Moderately, in 2

1. I was sink - ing deep in sin, far from the peace - ful shore,
2. All my heart to Him I give, ev - er to Him I'll cling;
3. Souls in dan - ger, look a - bove, Je - sus com - plete - ly saves;

ver - y deep - ly stained with - in, sink - ing to rise no more.
in His bless - ed pres - ence live, ev - er His prais - es sing.
He will lift you by His love out of the an - gry waves.

But the Mas - ter of the sea heard my de - spair - ing cry,
Love so might - y and so true mer - its my soul's best songs;
He's the Mas - ter of the sea, bil - lows His will o - bey;

from the wa - ters lift - ed me; now safe am I.
faith - ful, lov - ing serv - ice too, to Him be - longs.
He your Sav - ior wants to be, be saved to - day.

Chorus

Love lift - ed me! Love lift - ed me!

When noth - ing else could help, love lift - ed me.

Love lift - ed me! Love lift - ed me!

Play 3 times

When noth - ing else could help, love lift - ed me.

Standard Ukulele

D **A** **A7** **G**

Baritone Ukulele

D **A** **A7** **G**

Guitar

D **A** **A7** **G**

Mandolin

D **A** **A7** **G**

Banjo

D **A** **A7** **G**

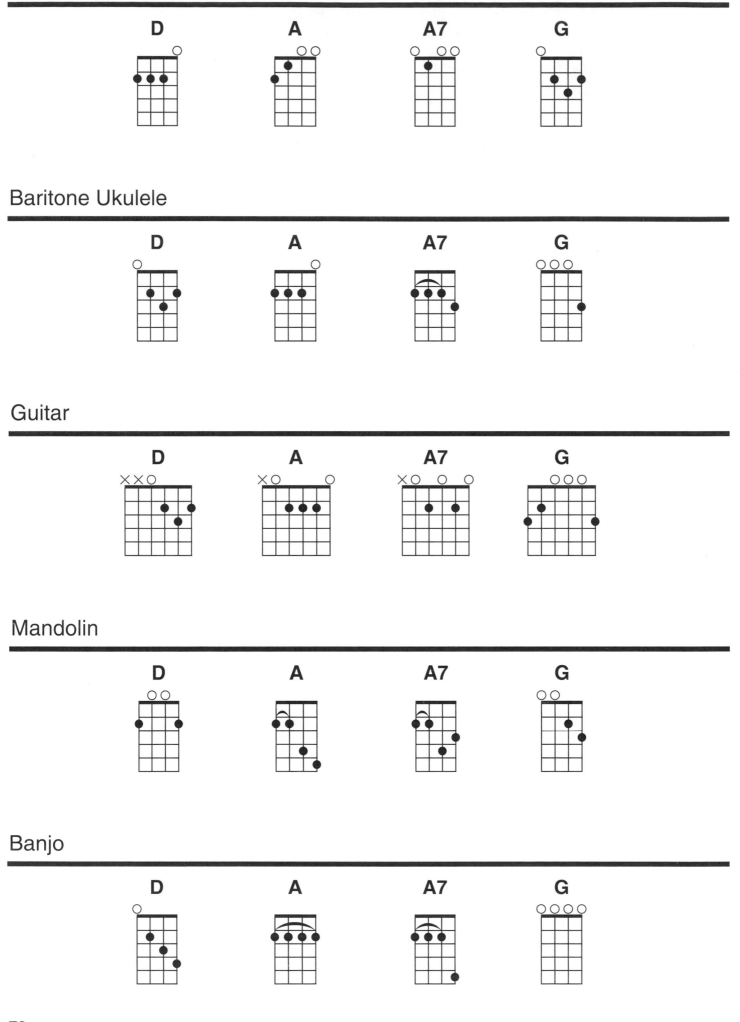

The Love of God
Words and Music by Frederick M. Lehman

Standard Ukulele

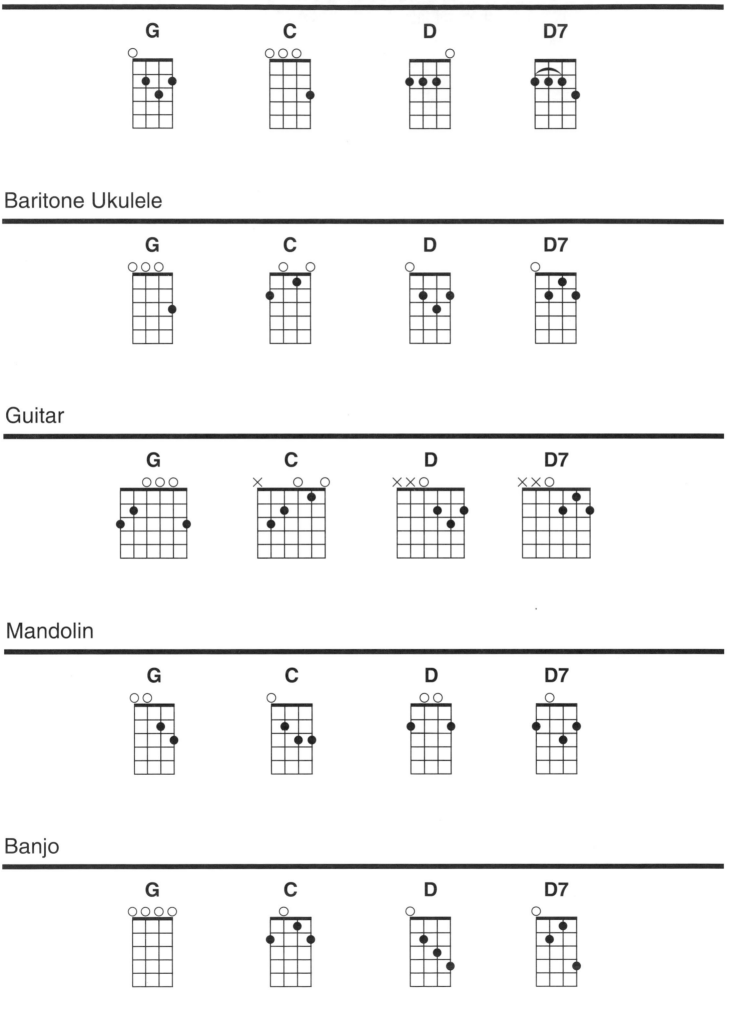

Baritone Ukulele

Guitar

Mandolin

Banjo

Near the Cross

Words by Fanny Crosby
Music by William H. Doane

1. Je - sus, keep me near the cross;
2. Near the cross a trem - bling soul,
3. Near the cross, O Lamb of God,
4. Near the cross I'll watch and wait,

there a pre - cious foun - tain.
love and mer - cy found me.
bring its scenes be - fore me.
hop - ing, trust - ing ev - er,

Free to all, a heal - ing stream
There the Bright and Morn - ing Star
Help me walk from day to day
till I reach the gold - en strand

flows from Cal - v'ry's moun - tain.
sheds its beams a - round me.
with its shad - ows o'er me.
just be - yond the riv - er.

Chorus

In the cross, in the cross be my

glo - ry ev - er, till my rap - tured

Play 4 times

soul shall find rest be - yond the riv - er.

Standard Ukulele

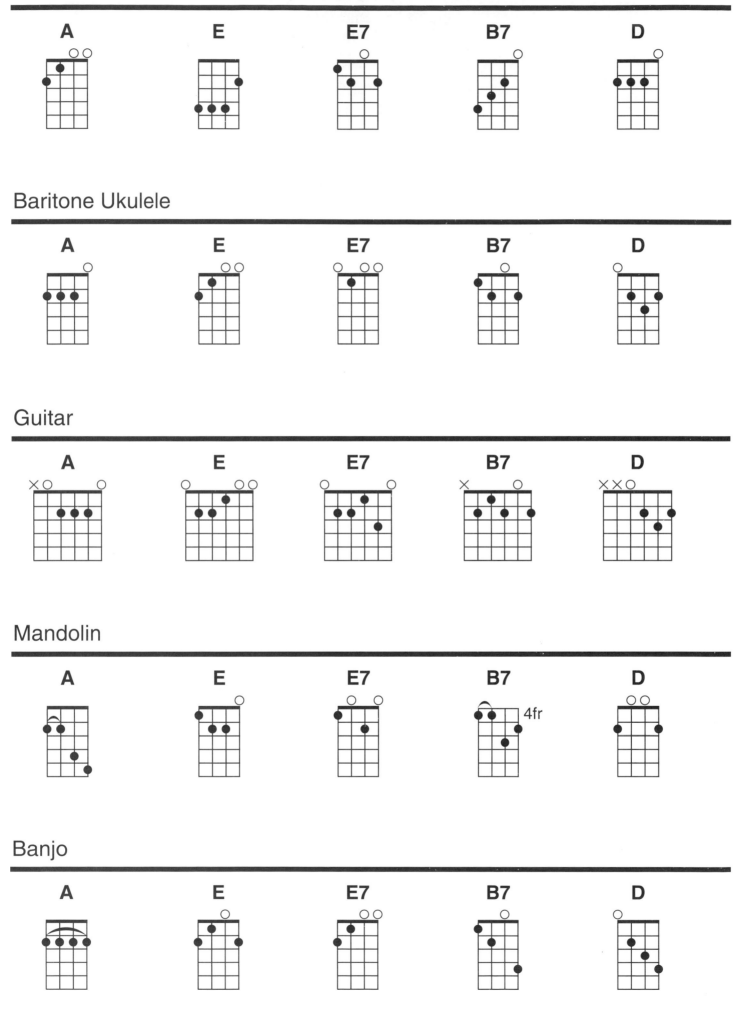

Baritone Ukulele

Guitar

Mandolin

Banjo

A New Name in Glory

Words and Music by C. Austin Miles

Standard Ukulele

D   **A7**

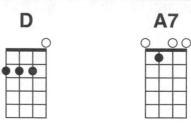

Baritone Ukulele

D   **A7**

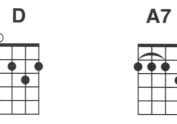

Guitar

D   **A7**

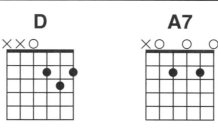

Mandolin

D   **A7**

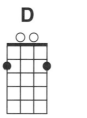

Banjo

D   **A7**

Nothing But the Blood

Words and Music by Robert Lowry

Standard Ukulele

G   D7   C

Baritone Ukulele

G   D7   C

Guitar

G   D7   C

Mandolin

G   D7   C

Banjo

G   D7   C

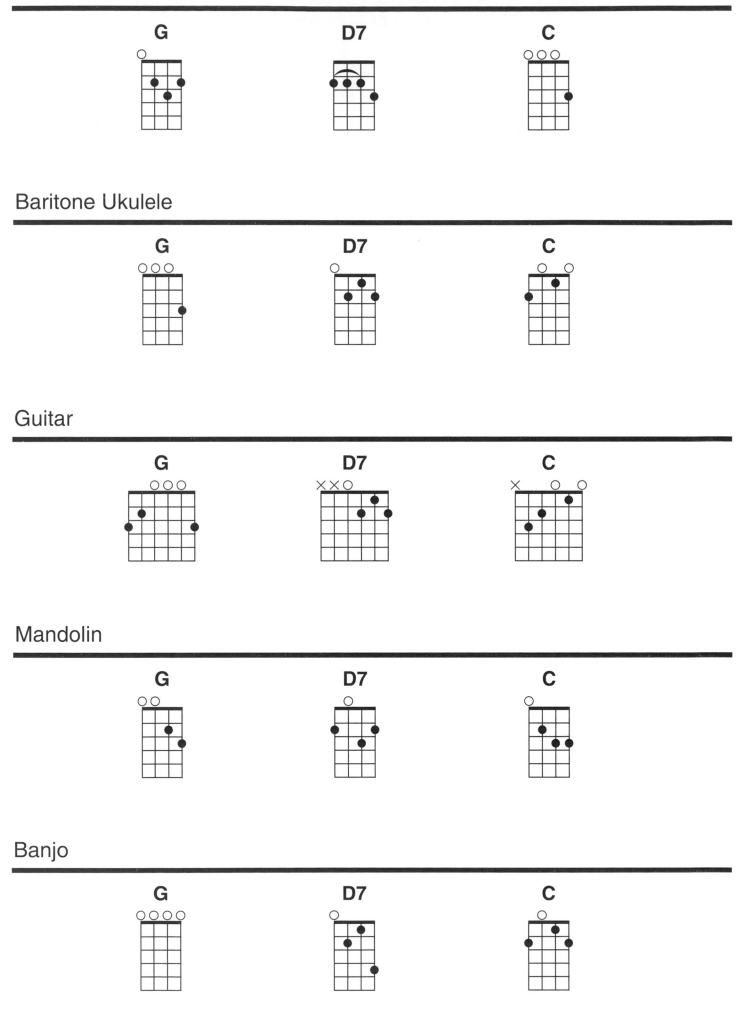

Oh, How I Love Jesus
(O How I Love Jesus)

Words by Frederick Whitfield
Traditional American Melody

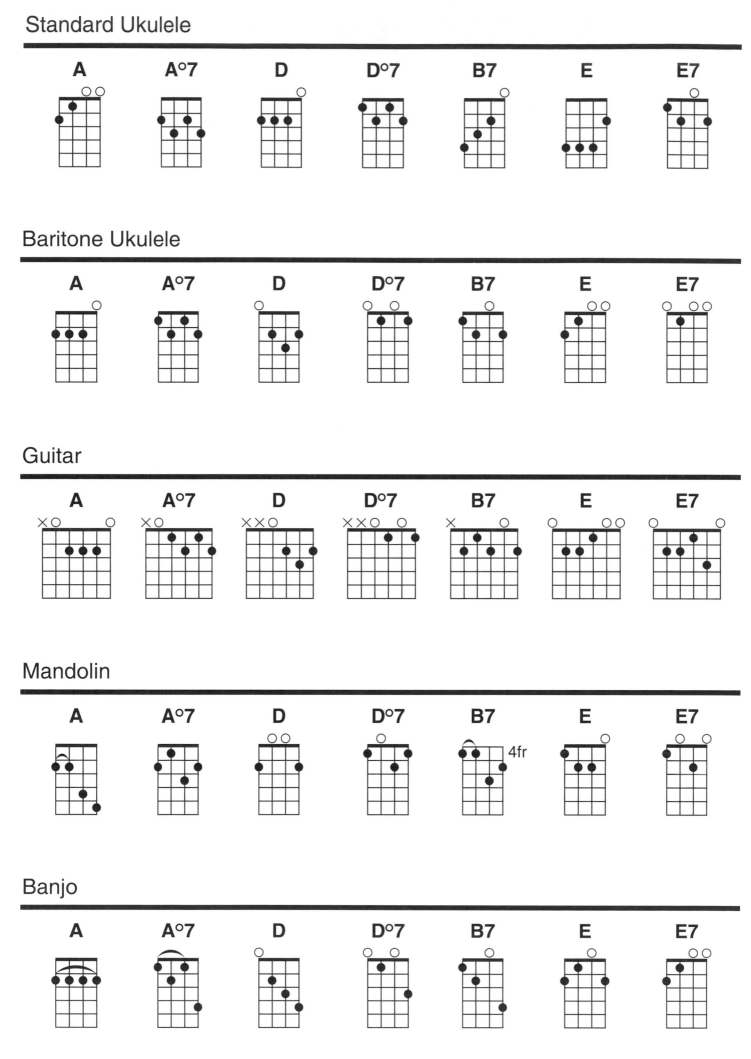

The Old Rugged Cross

Words and Music by Rev. George Bennard

Standard Ukulele

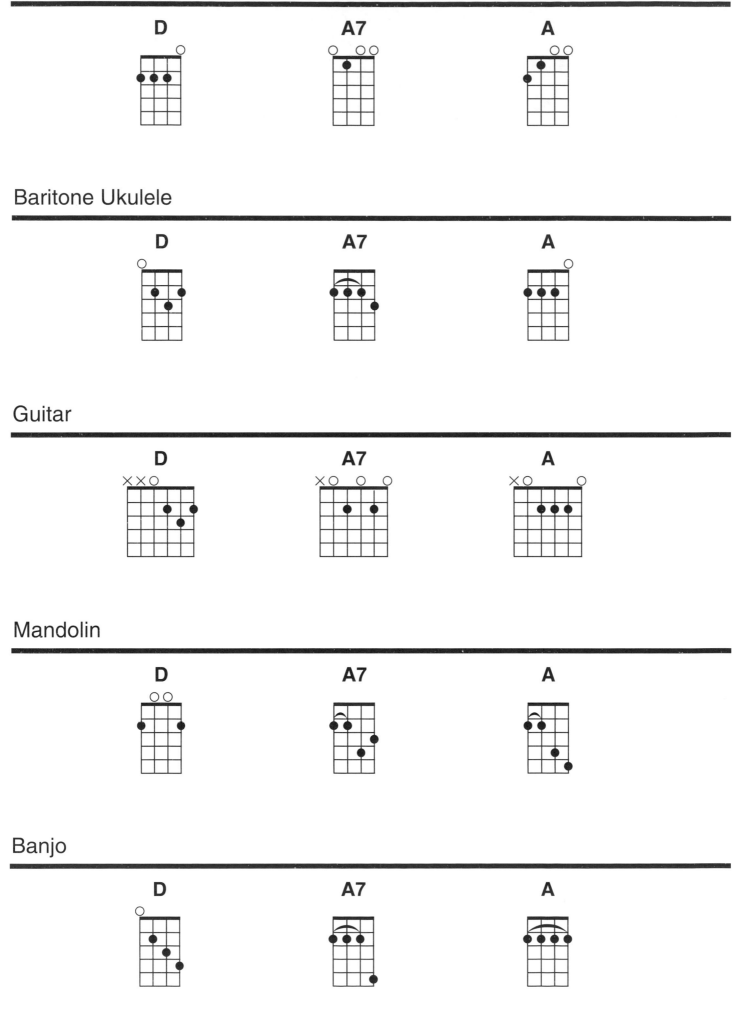

Baritone Ukulele

Guitar

Mandolin

Banjo

On Jordan's Stormy Banks

Words by Samuel Stennett
Traditional American Melody

Standard Ukulele

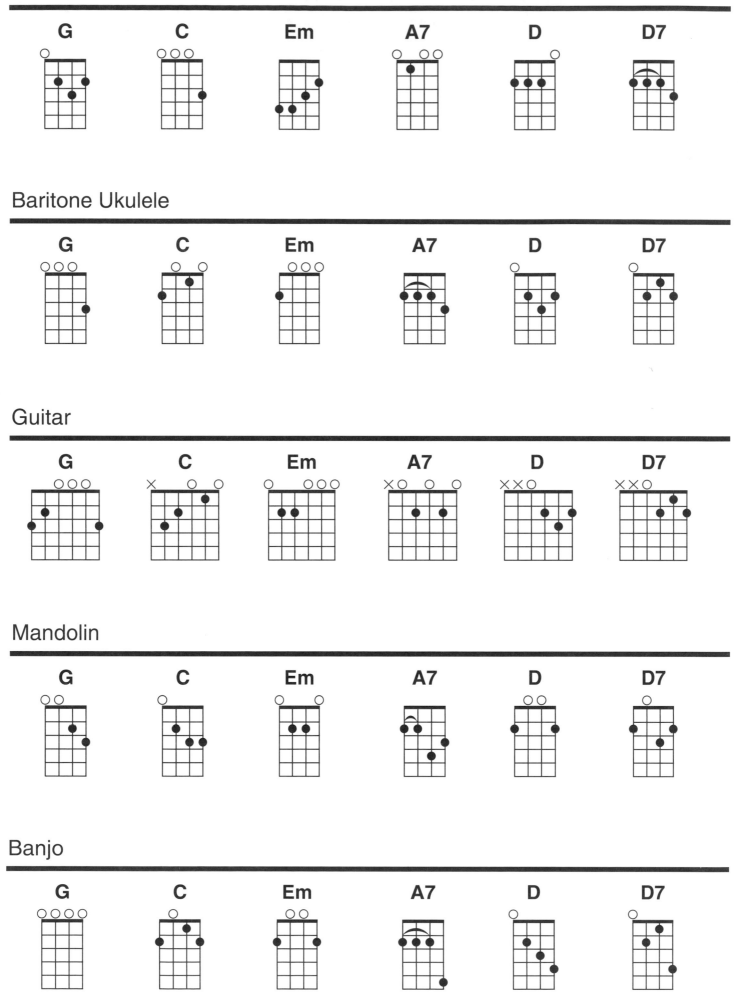

Baritone Ukulele

Guitar

Mandolin

Banjo

Precious Memories

Words and Music by J.B.F. Wright

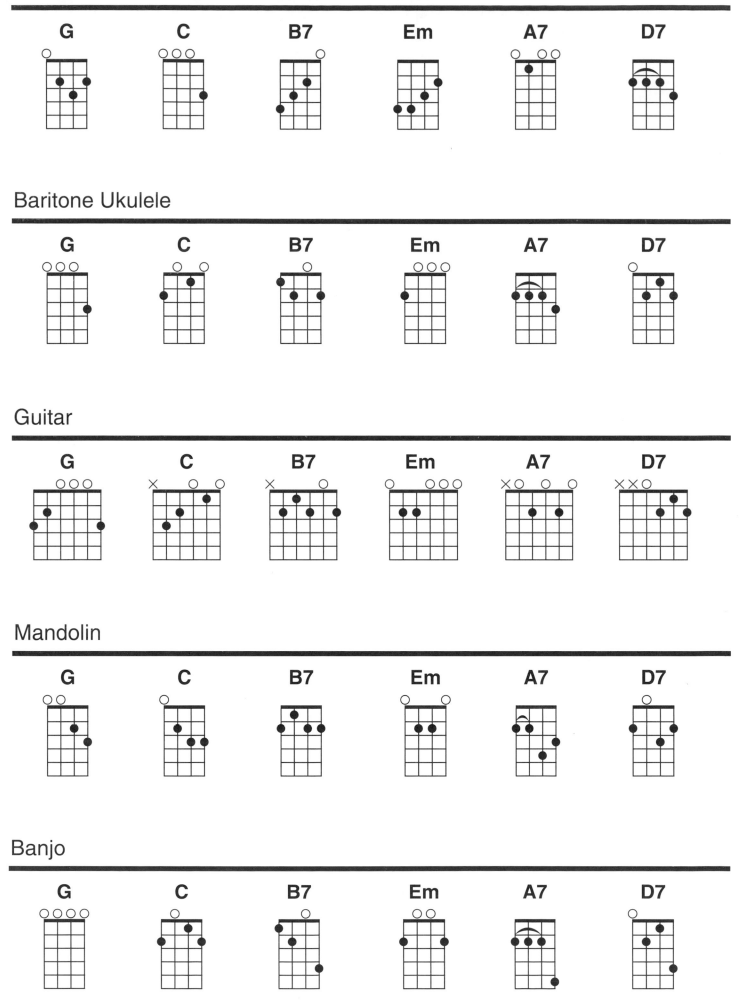

94

Revive Us Again

Words by William P. MacKay
Music by John J. Husband

1. We praise Thee, O God, for the Son of Thy
   praise Thee, O God, for Thy Spir - it of
   glo - ry and praise to the Lamb that was
   vive us a - gain, fill each heart with Thy

love, for _____ Je - sus who died and is
light, who has shown us our Sav - ior is and
slain, who has borne all our sins and has
love; may each soul be re - kin - dled with

Chorus

now gone a - bove.
scat - tered our night.
cleansed ev - 'ry stain.
fire from a - bove.

Hal - le - lu - jah, Thine the

glo - ry! Hal - le - lu - jah, a - men! Hal - le - lu - jah, Thine the

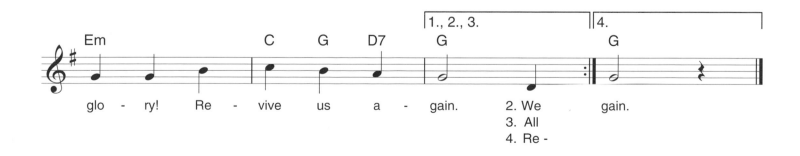

glo - ry! Re - vive us a - gain.   2. We   gain.
                                   3. All
                                   4. Re -

Standard Ukulele

A   D   E7

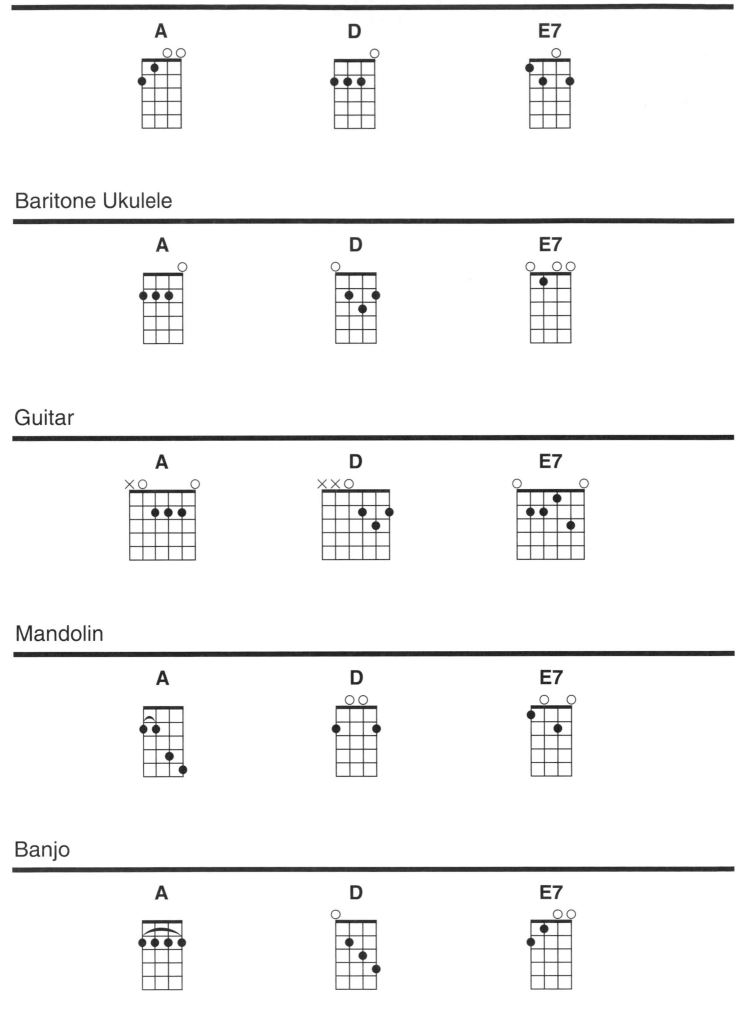

Baritone Ukulele

A   D   E7

Guitar

A   D   E7

Mandolin

A   D   E7

Banjo

A   D   E7

Rock of Ages

Words by Augustus M. Toplady
V.1,2 altered by Thomas Cotterill
Music by Thomas Hastings

Standard Ukulele

G **D7**

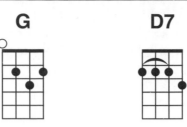

Baritone Ukulele

G **D7**

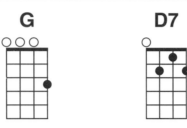

Guitar

G **D7**

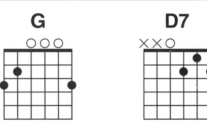

Mandolin

G **D7**

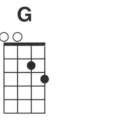

Banjo

G **D7**

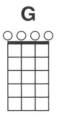 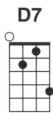

Send the Light

Words and Music by Charles H. Gabriel

Standard Ukulele

D   A7   A   G

Baritone Ukulele

D   A7   A   G

Guitar

D   A7   A   G

Mandolin

D   A7   A   G

Banjo

D   A7   A   G

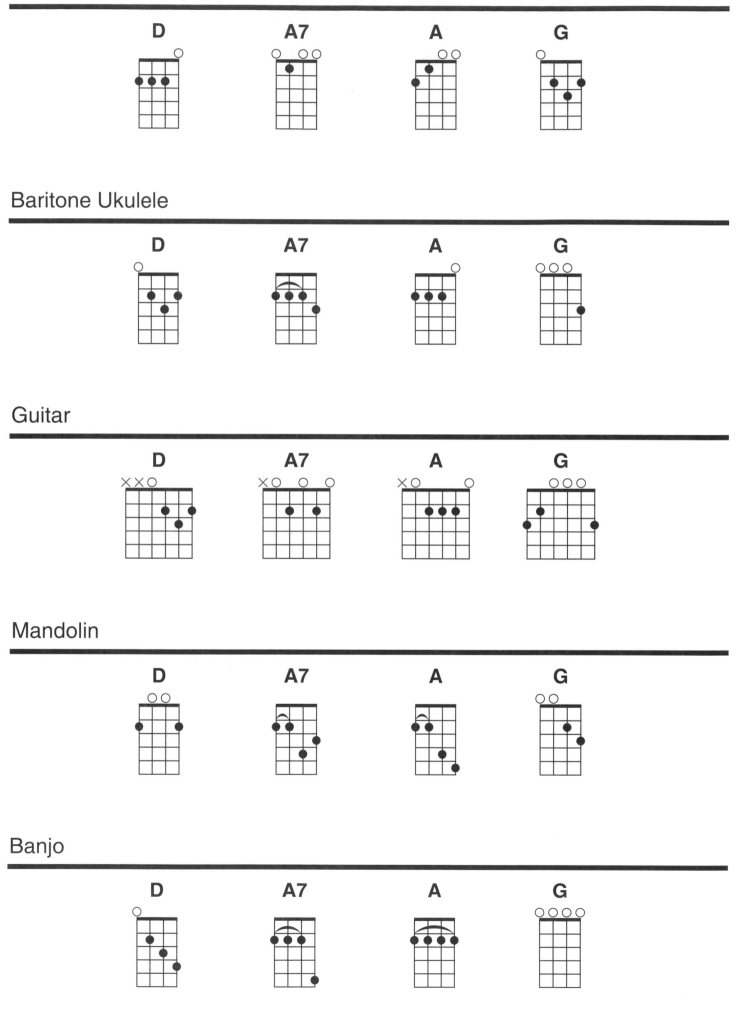

Shall We Gather at the River?

Words and Music by Robert Lowry

Standard Ukulele

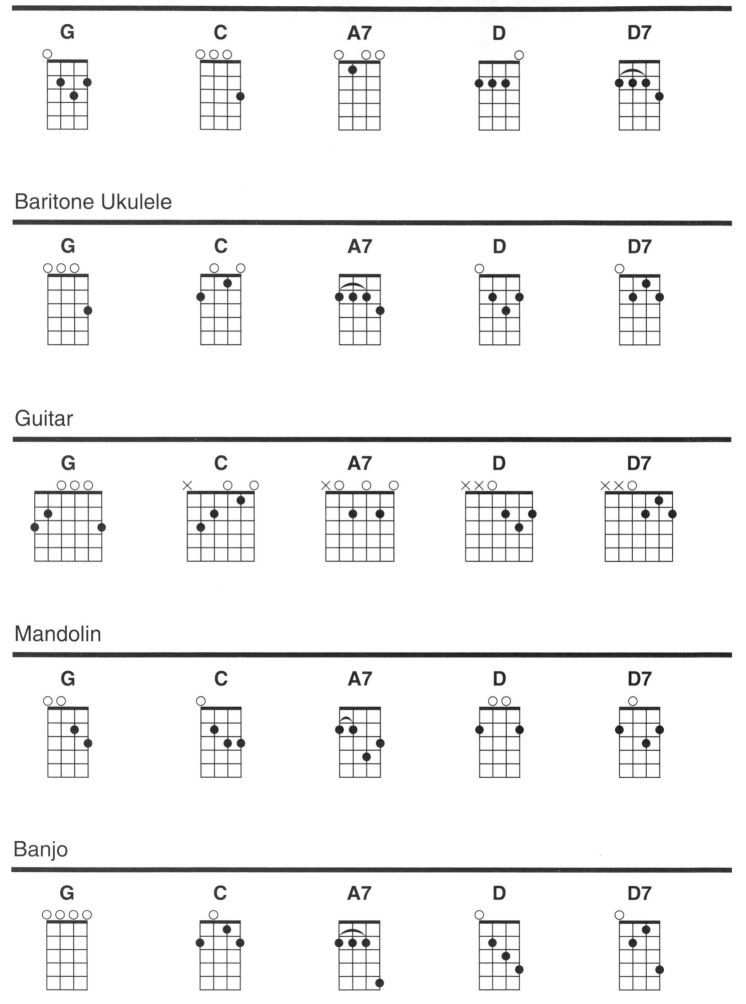

Baritone Ukulele

Guitar

Mandolin

Banjo

Since Jesus Came Into My Heart

Words by Rufus H. McDaniel
Music by Charles H. Gabriel

Standard Ukulele

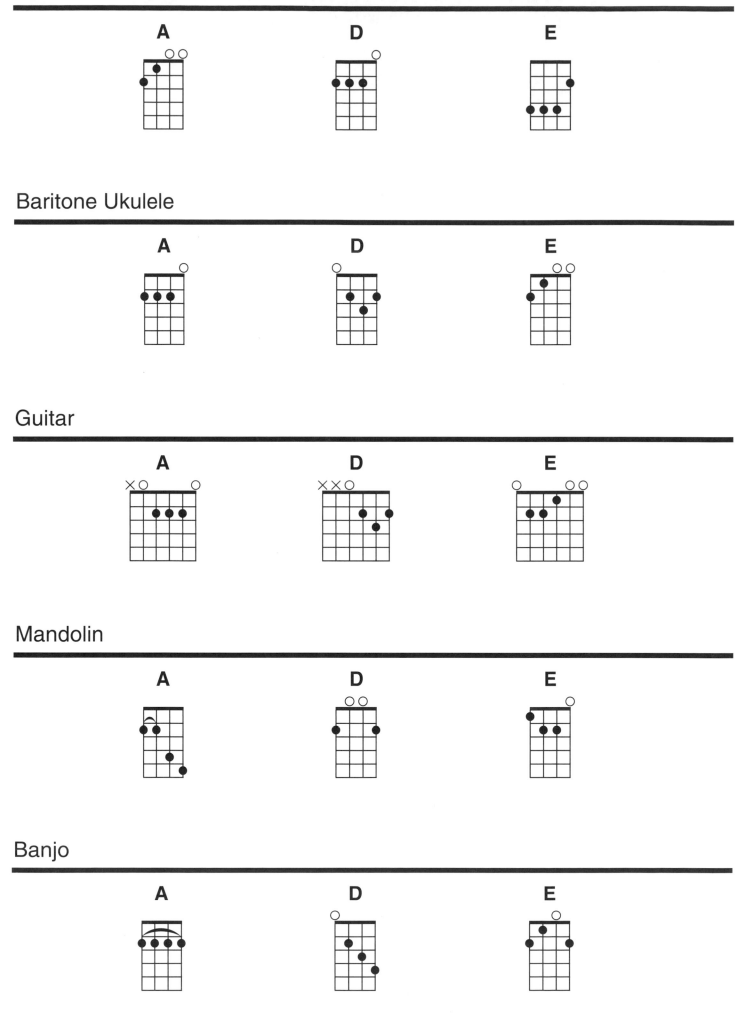

Baritone Ukulele

Guitar

Mandolin

Banjo

Standing on the Promises

Words and Music by R. Kelso Carter

1. Stand - ing on the prom - is - es of Christ my King,
2. Stand - ing on the prom - is - es that can - not fail,
3. Stand - ing on the prom - is - es of Christ the Lord,
4. Stand - ing on the prom - is - es I can - not fall,

through e - ter - nal ag - es let His prais - es ring. Glo - ry in the high - est, I will
when the howl - ing storms of doubt and fear as - sail. By the liv - ing word of God I
bound to Him e - ter - nal - ly by love's strong cord. O - ver - com - ing dai - ly with the
lis - t'ning ev - 'ry mo - ment to the Spir - it's call. Rest - ing in my Sav - ior as my

shout and sing, stand - ing on the prom - is - es of God.
shall pre - vail, stand - ing on the prom - is - es of God.
Spir - it's sword, stand - ing on the prom - is - es of God.
all in all, stand - ing on the prom - is - es of God.

Chorus

Stand - ing, stand - ing, stand - ing on the prom - is - es of

God my Sav - ior. Stand - ing, stand - ing, I'm

Play 4 times

stand - ing on the prom - is - es of God.

Standard Ukulele

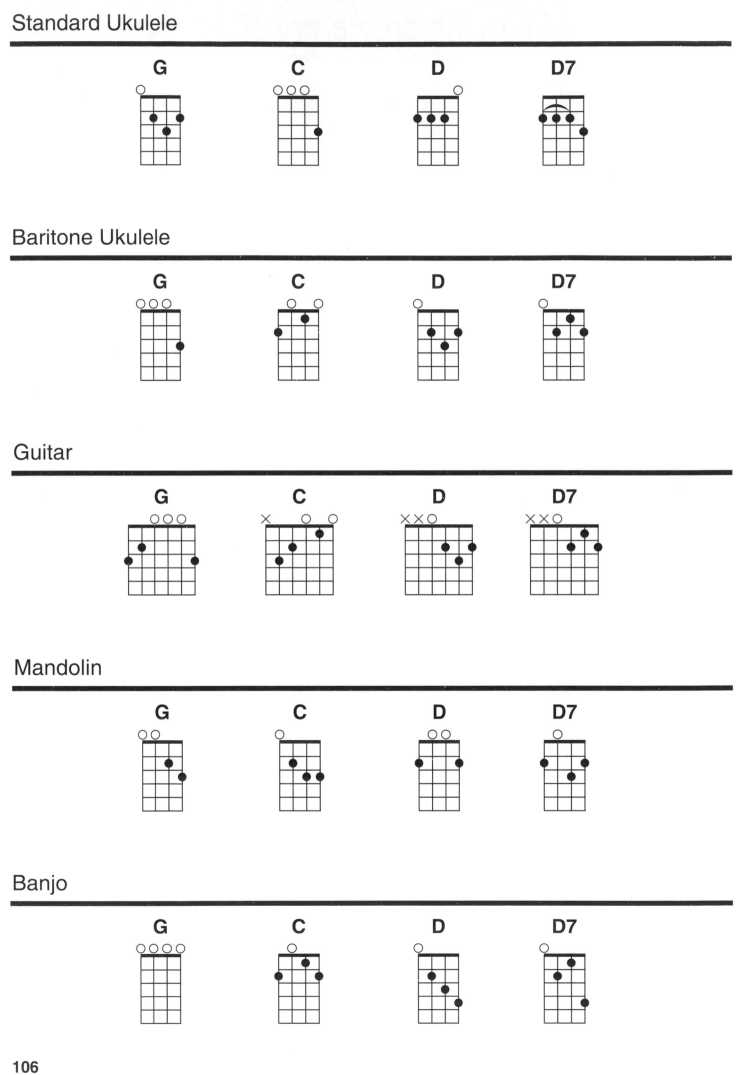

Baritone Ukulele

Guitar

Mandolin

Banjo

Sweet By and By

Words by Sanford Fillmore Bennett
Music by Joseph P. Webster

Standard Ukulele

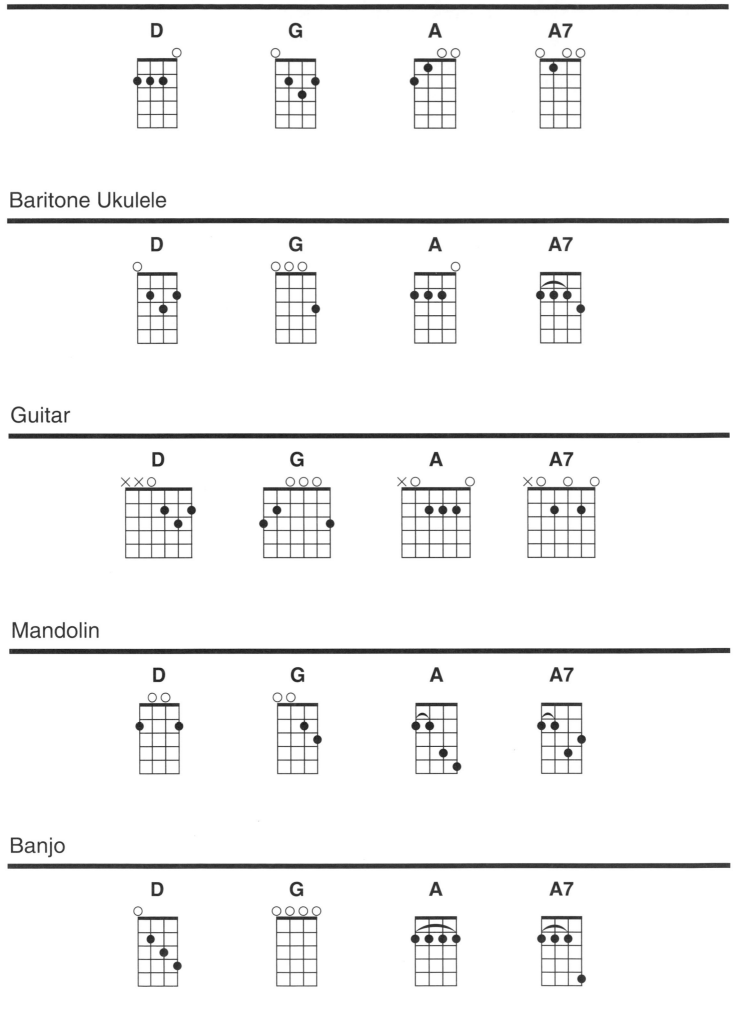

Baritone Ukulele

Guitar

Mandolin

Banjo

Sweet Hour of Prayer

Words by William W. Walford
Music by William B. Bradbury

Standard Ukulele

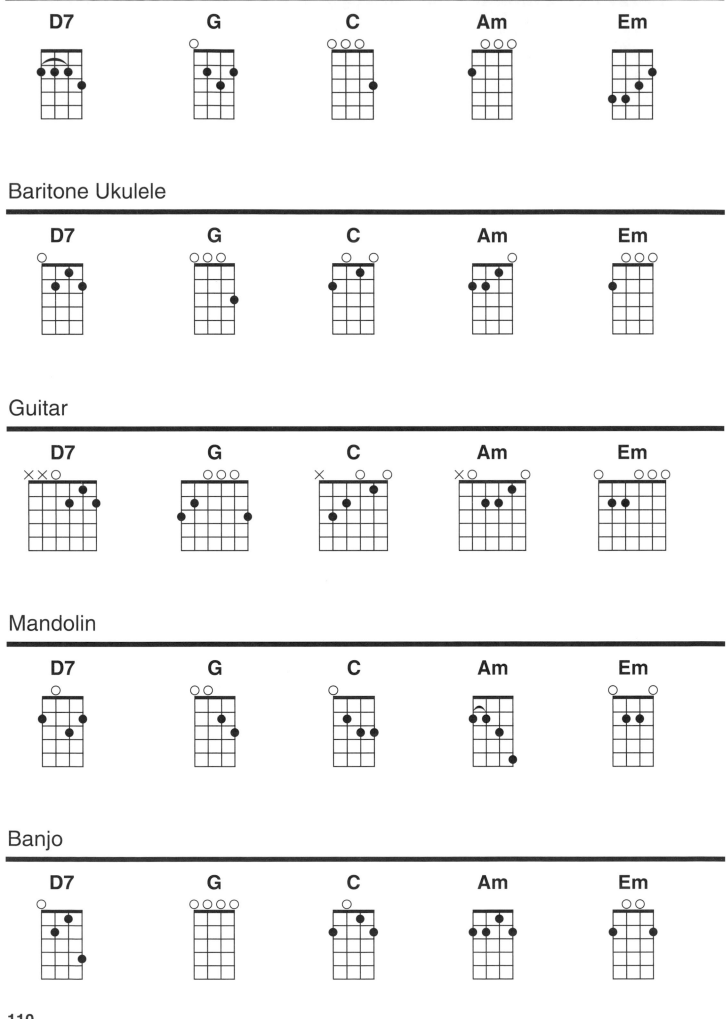

Baritone Ukulele

Guitar

Mandolin

Banjo

There Is a Balm in Gilead

African-American Spiritual

Standard Ukulele

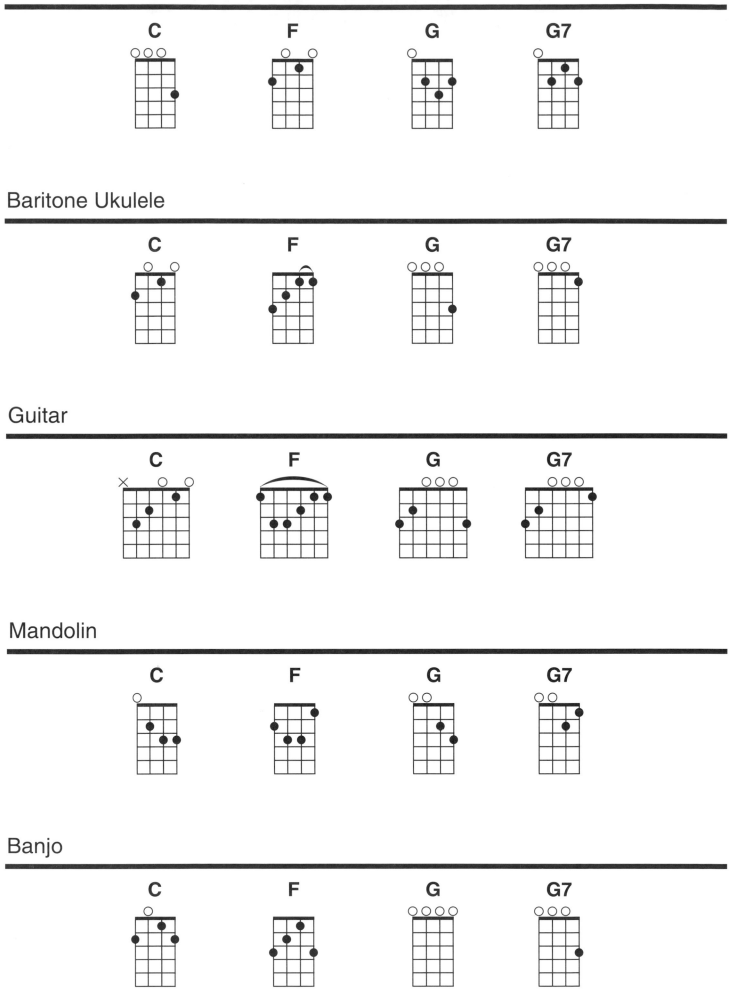

Baritone Ukulele

Guitar

Mandolin

Banjo

There Is a Fountain

Words by William Cowper
Traditional American Melody

Standard Ukulele

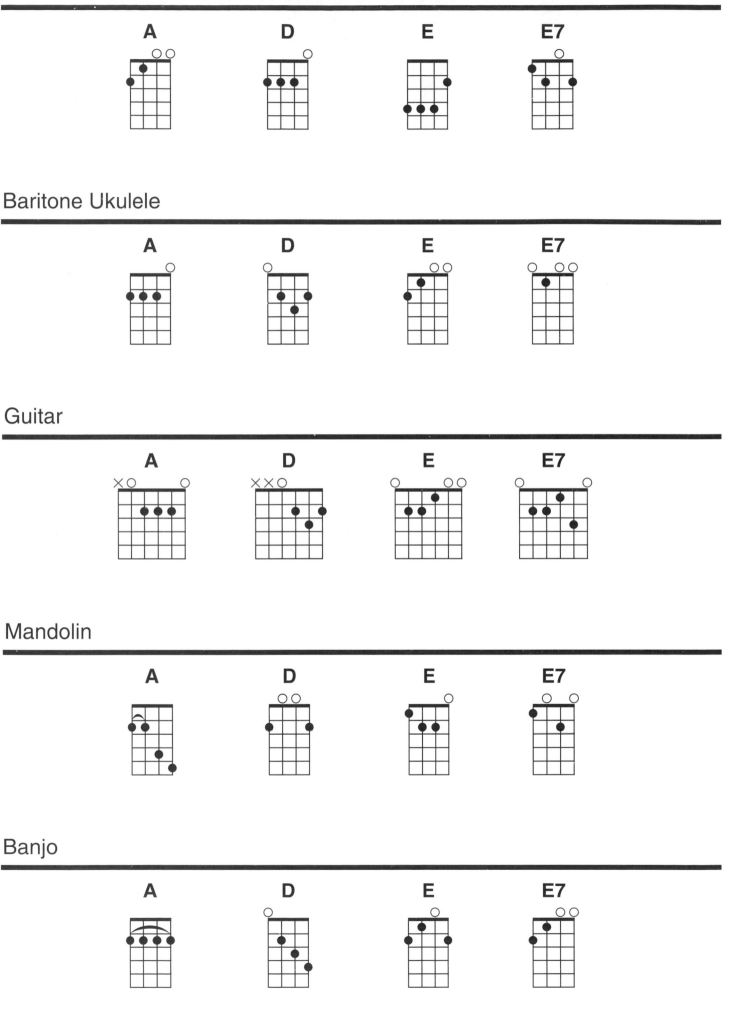

A	D	E	E7

Baritone Ukulele

A	D	E	E7

Guitar

A	D	E	E7

Mandolin

A	D	E	E7

Banjo

A	D	E	E7

There Is Power in the Blood

Words and Music by Lewis E. Jones

Standard Ukulele

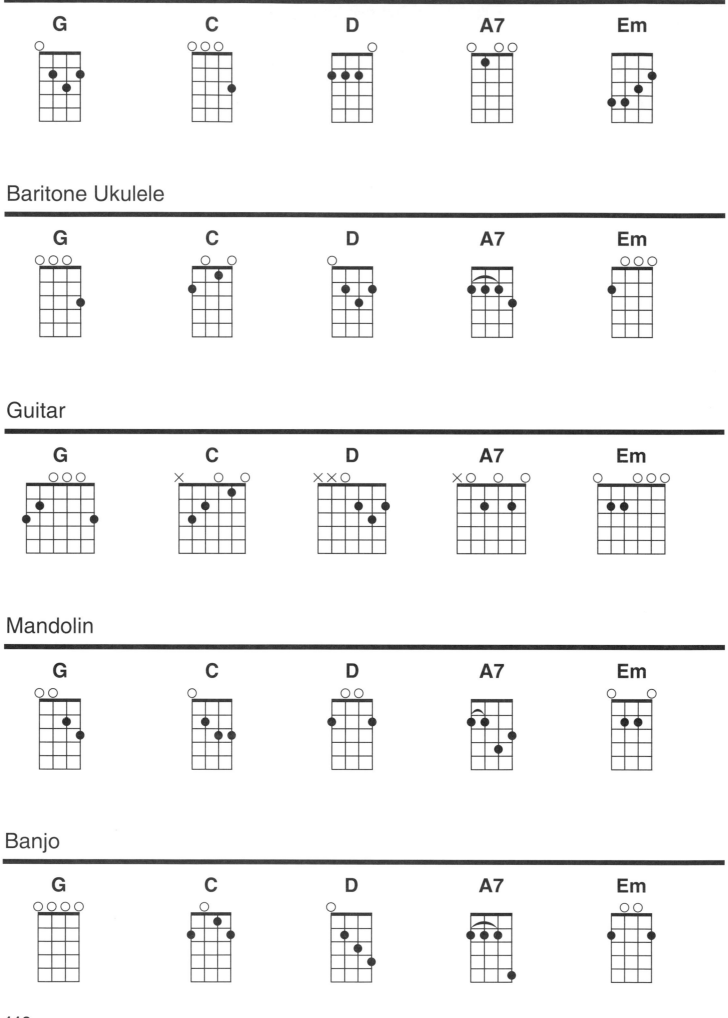

G **C** **D** **A7** **Em**

Baritone Ukulele

G **C** **D** **A7** **Em**

Guitar

G **C** **D** **A7** **Em**

Mandolin

G **C** **D** **A7** **Em**

Banjo

G **C** **D** **A7** **Em**

'Tis So Sweet to Trust in Jesus

Words by Louisa M.R. Stead
Music by William J. Kirkpatrick

Verse
Moderately

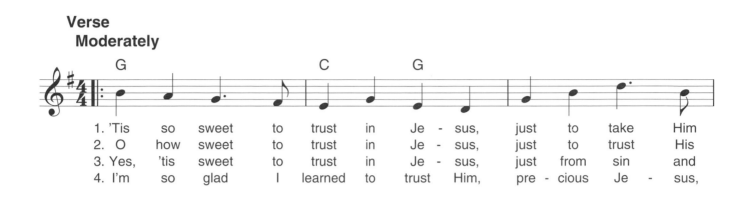

1. 'Tis so sweet to trust in Je - sus, just to take Him
2. O how sweet to trust in Je - sus, just to trust His
3. Yes, 'tis sweet to trust in Je - sus, just from sin and
4. I'm so glad I learned to trust Him, pre - cious Je - sus,

at His word, just to rest up - on His prom - ise,
cleans - ing blood, just in sim - ple faith to plunge me
self to cease, just from Je - sus sim - ply tak - ing
Sav - ior, Friend, and I know that He is with me,

Chorus

just to know, "Thus saith the Lord." Je - sus, Je - sus,
'neath the heal - ing, cleans - ing flood.
life and rest and joy and peace.
will be with me to the end.

how I trust Him! How I've proved Him o'er and o'er!

Play 4 times

Je - sus, Je - sus, pre - cious Je - sus! O for grace to trust Him more!

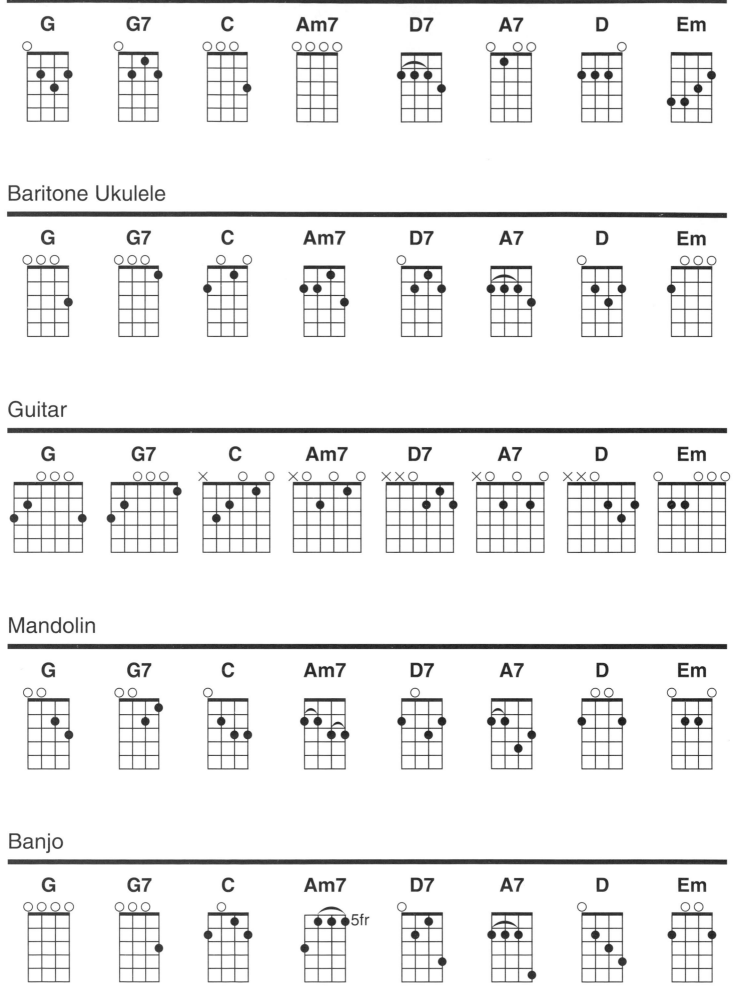

Turn Your Eyes Upon Jesus

Words and Music by Helen H. Lemmel

Standard Ukulele

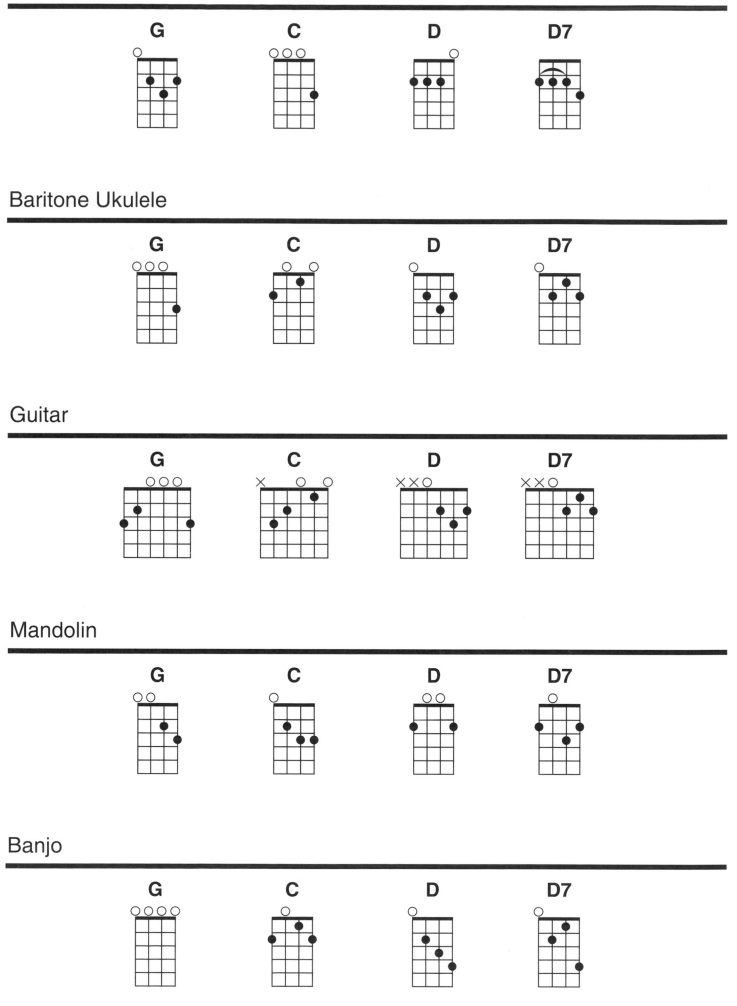

Baritone Ukulele

Guitar

Mandolin

Banjo

The Unclouded Day

Words and Music by J.K. Alwood

Standard Ukulele

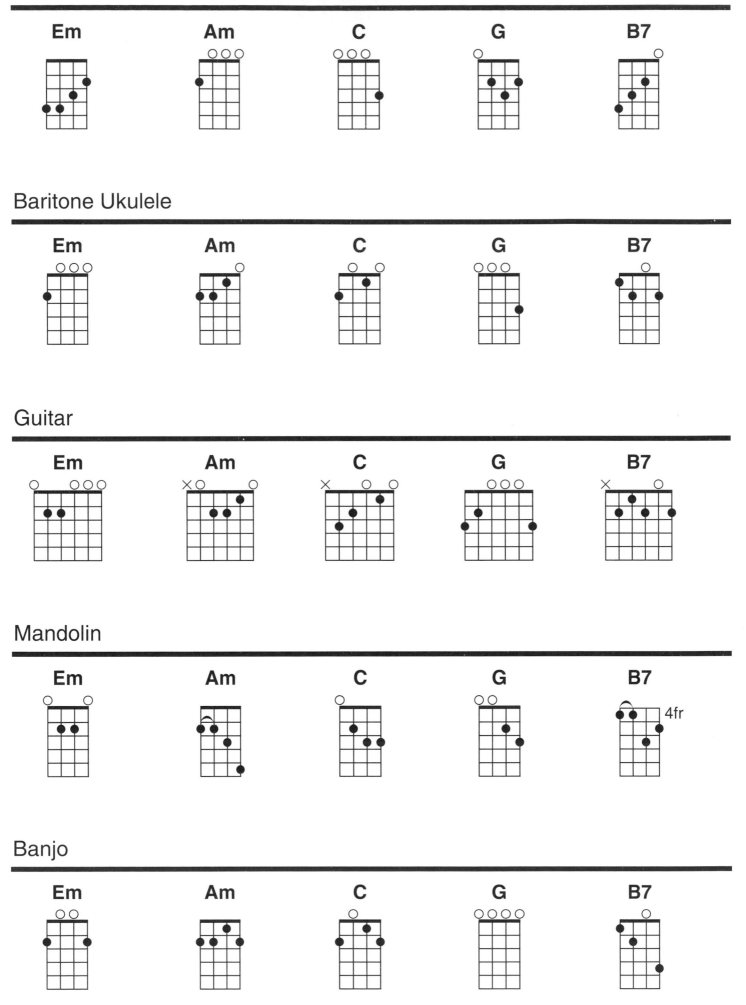

Baritone Ukulele

Guitar

Mandolin

Banjo

Wayfaring Stranger

Southern American Folk Hymn

Standard Ukulele

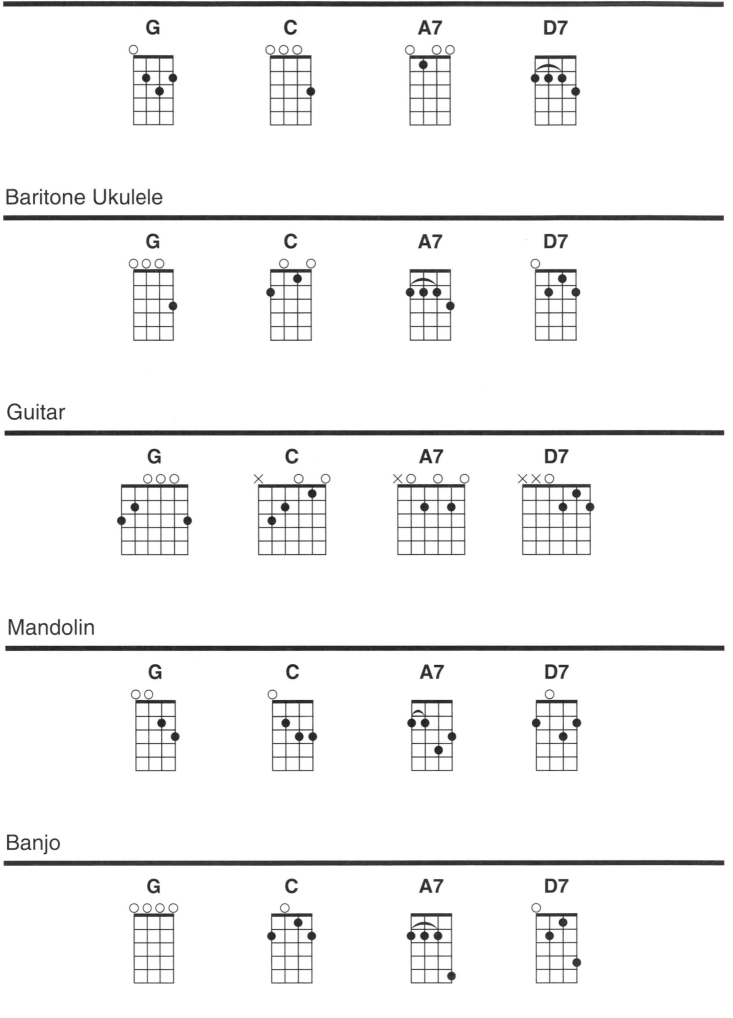

Baritone Ukulele

Guitar

Mandolin

Banjo

We'll Understand It Better By and By

Words and Music by Charles A. Tindley

Standard Ukulele

G C D7 A7

Baritone Ukulele

G C D7 A7

Guitar

G C D7 A7

Mandolin

G C D7 A7

Banjo

G C D7 A7

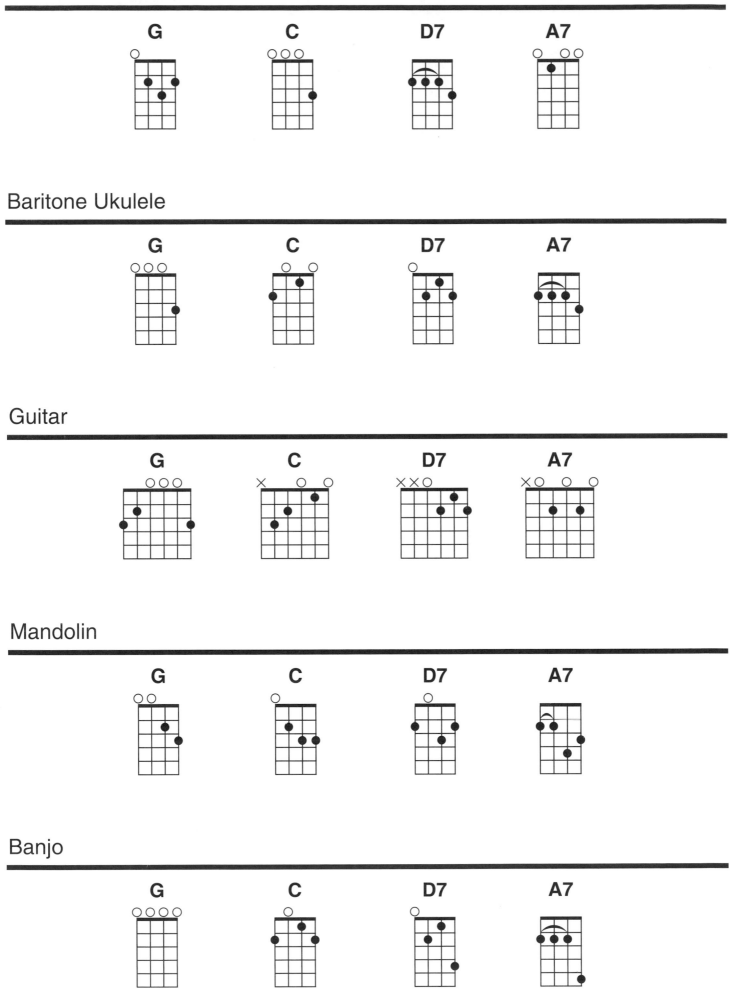

What a Friend We Have in Jesus

Words by Joseph M. Scriven
Music by Charles C. Converse

Standard Ukulele

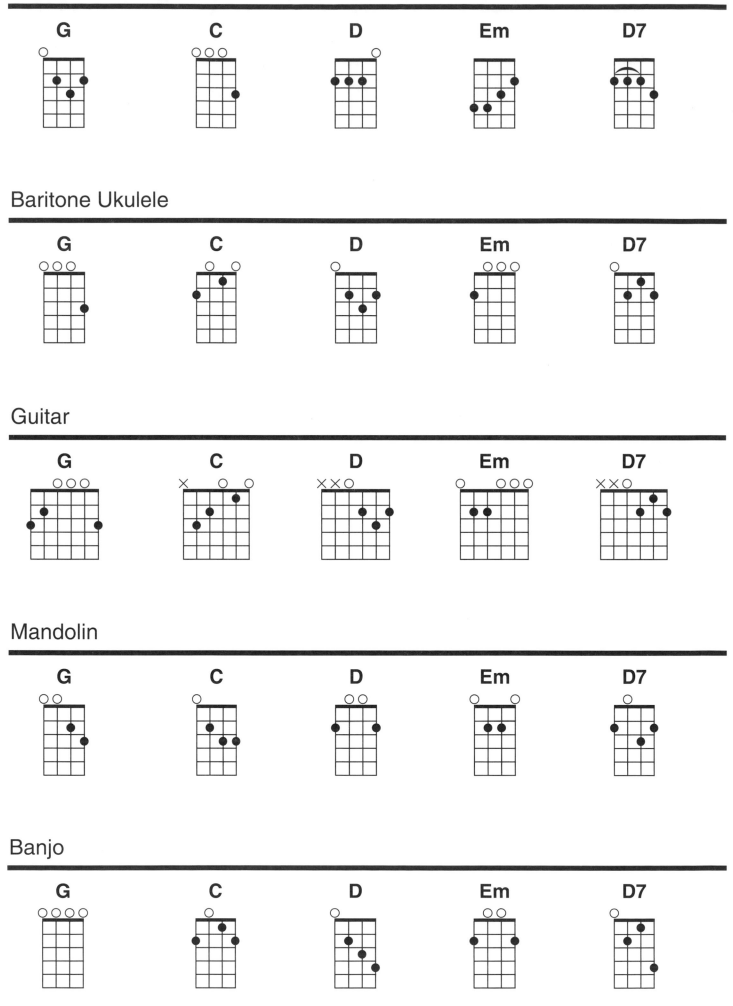

Baritone Ukulele

Guitar

Mandolin

Banjo

When I Can Read My Title Clear

Words by Isaac Watts
Traditional American Melody attributed to Joseph C. Lowry

Standard Ukulele

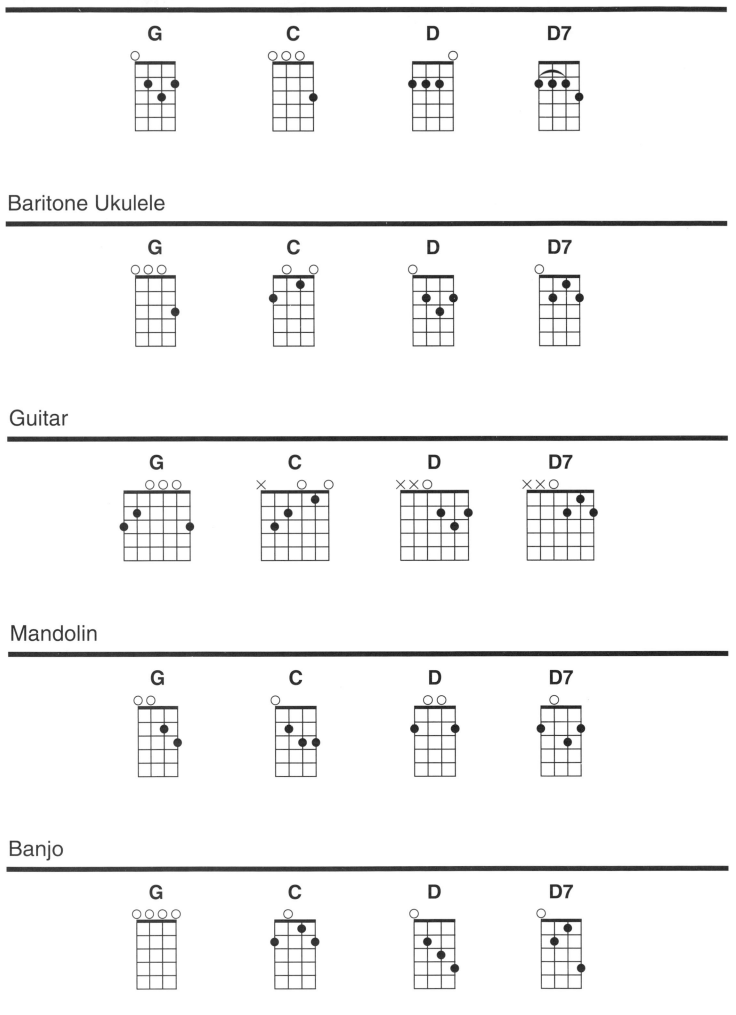

Baritone Ukulele

Guitar

Mandolin

Banjo

When the Roll Is Called Up Yonder

Words and Music by James M. Black

Standard Ukulele

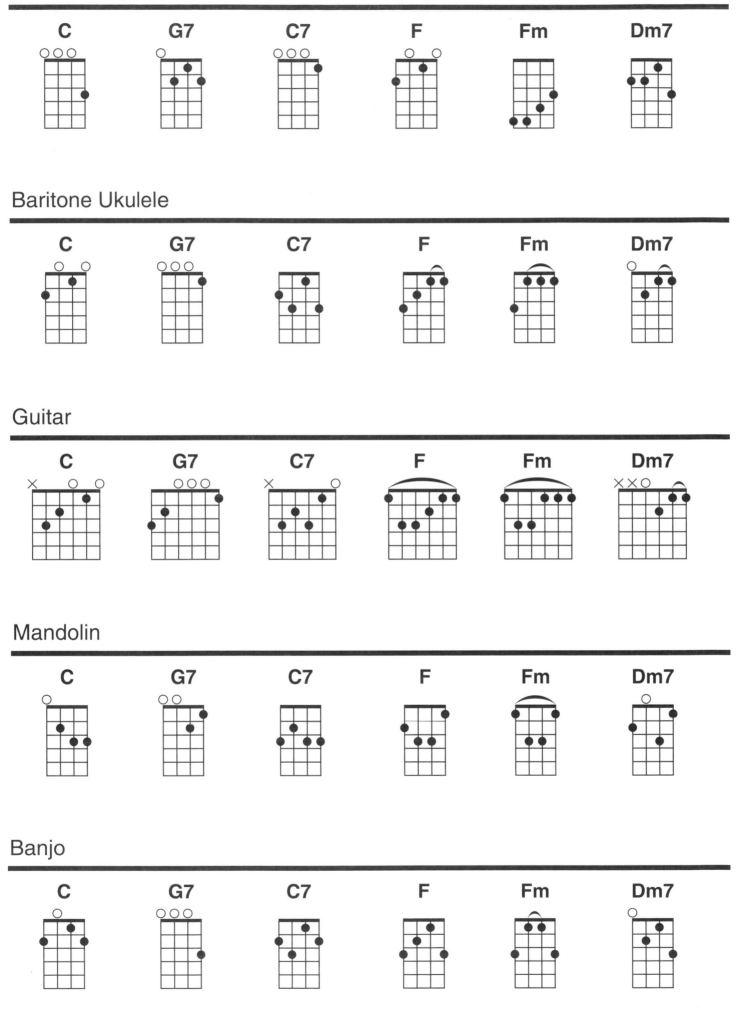

C G7 C7 F Fm Dm7

Baritone Ukulele

C G7 C7 F Fm Dm7

Guitar

C G7 C7 F Fm Dm7

Mandolin

C G7 C7 F Fm Dm7

Banjo

C G7 C7 F Fm Dm7

When the Saints Go Marching In

Words by Katherine E. Purvis
Music by James M. Black

Standard Ukulele

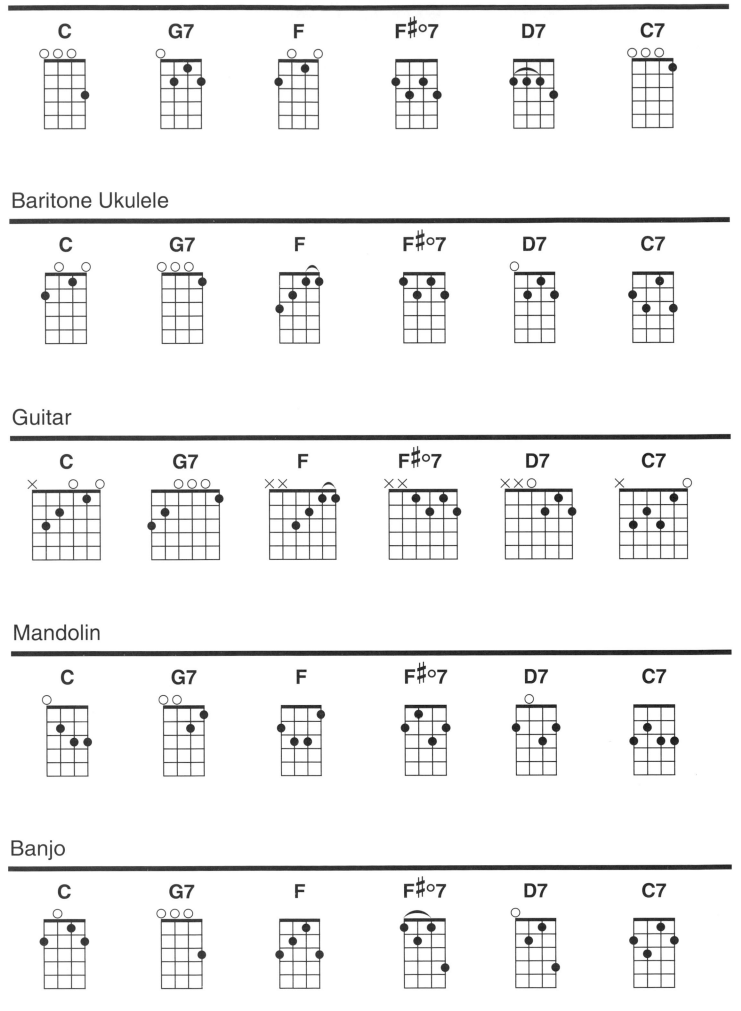

Baritone Ukulele

Guitar

Mandolin

Banjo

When We All Get to Heaven

Words by Eliza E. Hewitt
Music by Emily D. Wilson

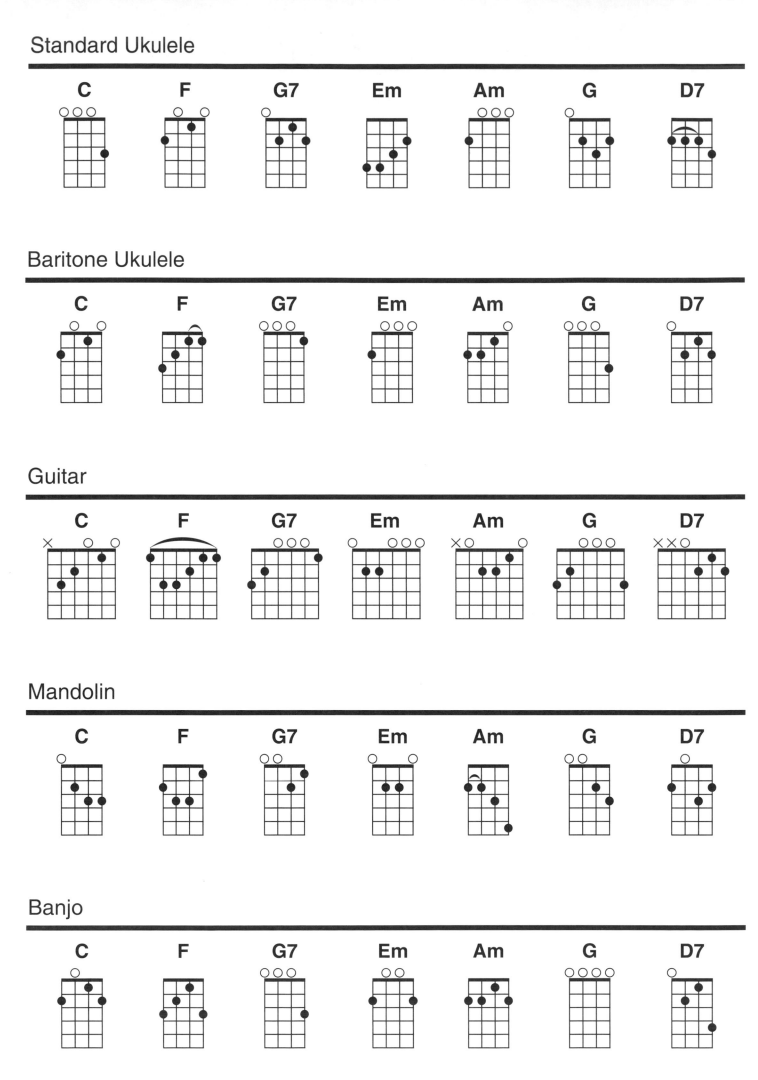

Whispering Hope

Words and Music by Alice Hawthorne

Standard Ukulele

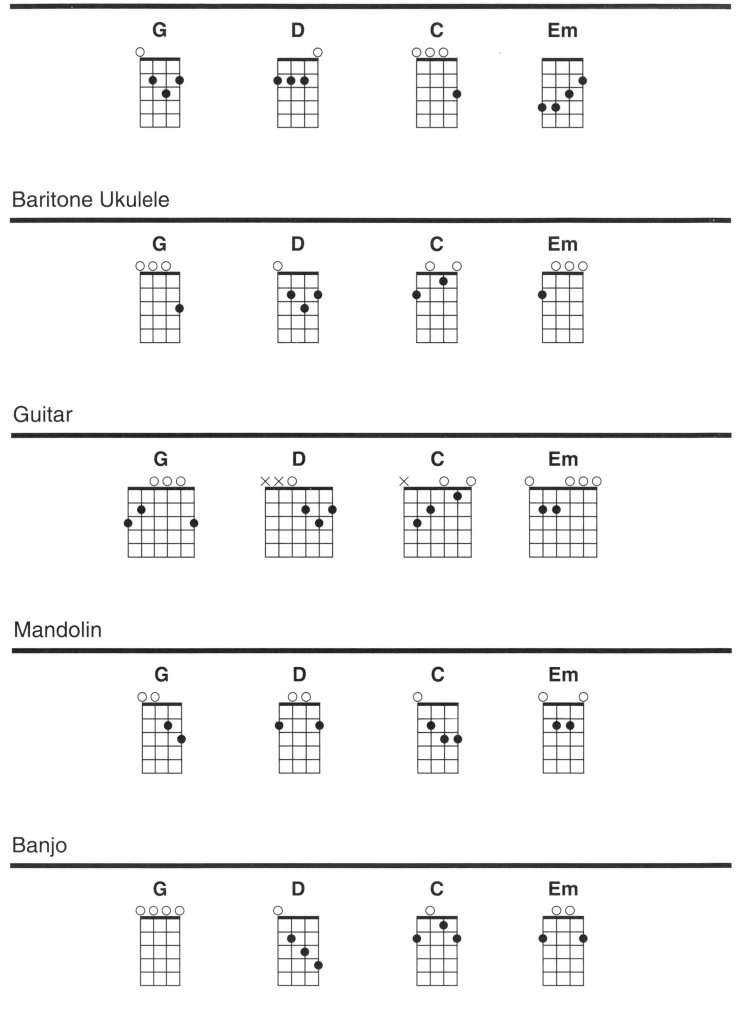

Baritone Ukulele

Guitar

Mandolin

Banjo

Whiter than Snow

Words by James L. Nicholson
Music by William G. Fischer

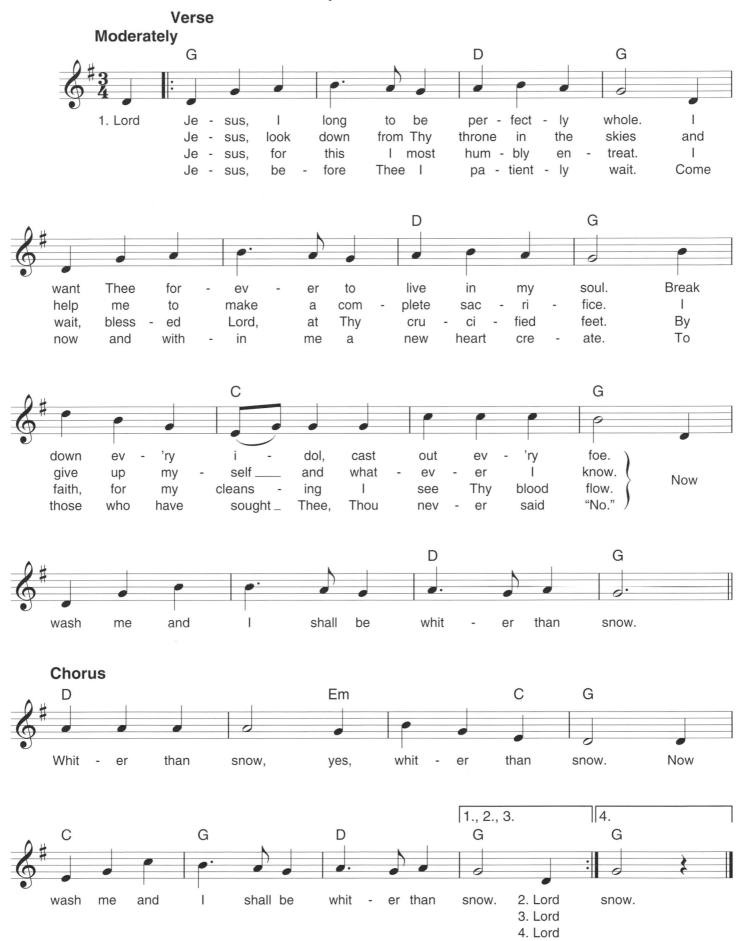

Verse
Moderately

1. Lord Je - sus, I long to be per - fect - ly whole. I
Je - sus, look down from Thy throne in the skies and
Je - sus, for this I most hum - bly en - treat. I
Je - sus, be - fore Thee I pa - tient - ly wait. Come

want Thee for - ev - er to live in my soul. Break
help me to make a com - plete sac - ri - fice. I
wait, bless - ed Lord, at Thy cru - ci - fied feet. By
now and with - in me a new heart cre - ate. To

down ev - 'ry i - dol, cast out ev - 'ry foe.
give up my - self ___ and what - ev - er I know. Now
faith, for my cleans - ing I see Thy blood flow.
those who have sought ___ Thee, Thou nev - er said "No."

wash me and I shall be whit - er than snow.

Chorus

Whit - er than snow, yes, whit - er than snow. Now

wash me and I shall be whit - er than snow. 2. Lord snow.
3. Lord
4. Lord

1., 2., 3.   4.

Standard Ukulele

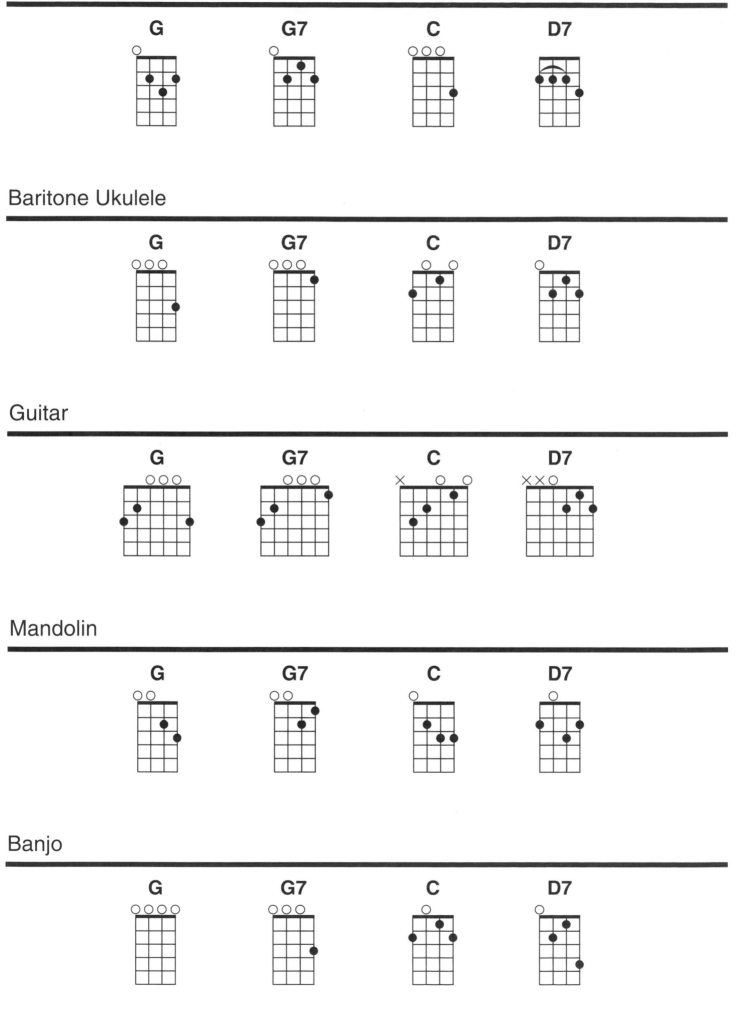

Baritone Ukulele

Guitar

Mandolin

Banjo

Will the Circle Be Unbroken

Words by Ada R. Habershon
Music by Charles H. Gabriel

Standard Ukulele

Baritone Ukulele

Guitar

Mandolin

Banjo

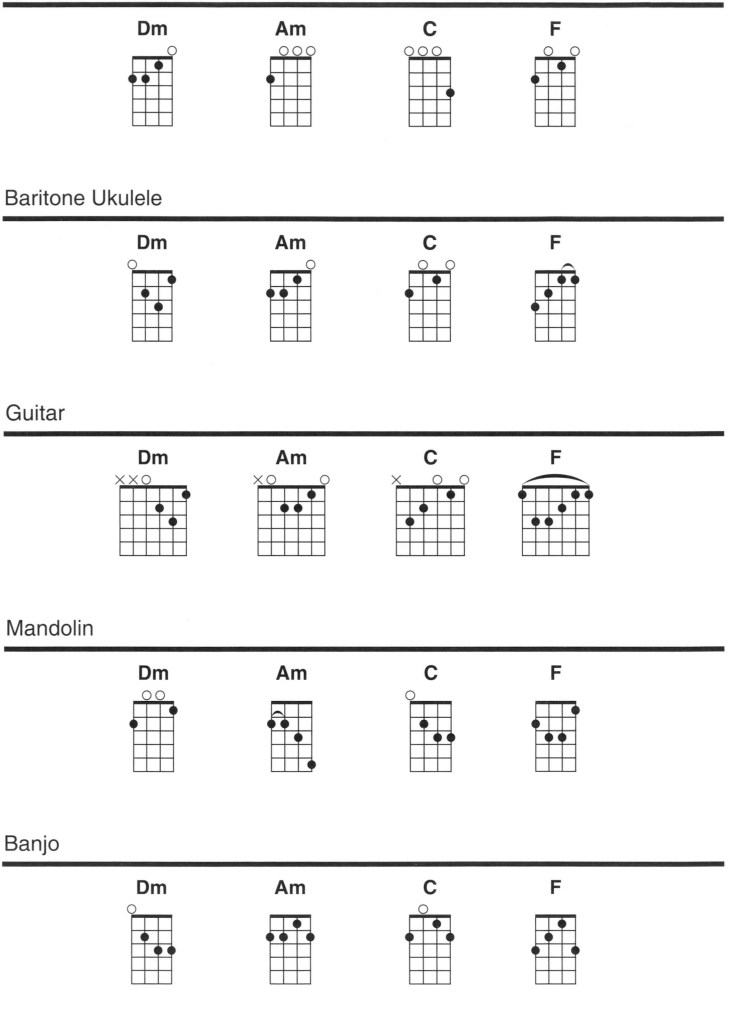

Wondrous Love

Southern American Folk Hymn

Tuning

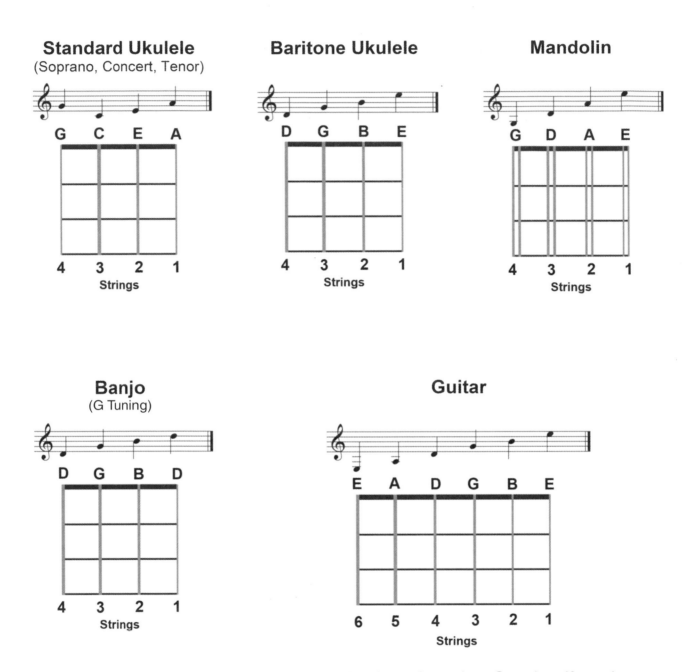

All banjo chord formations illustrated in this book are based on G tuning. If an alternate tuning is used the banjo player can read the chord letters for the songs and disregard the diagrams.